We the People

Teacher's Guide

Level II
Middle School

Center for Civic Education 5146 Douglas Fir Road • Calabasas, CA 91302 • (818) 591-9321

Directed by the
Center for Civic Education
and
Funded by the
U.S. Department of Education by act of Congress
Established 1987 under the
Commission on the Bicentennial of the United States Constitution

Cover: "Stump Speaking," George Caleb Bingham
Art Collection of The Boatmen's National Bank of St. Louis

Copyright © Center for Civic Education 1988
Twelfth Printing 1996

The U.S. Department of Education disclaims the responsibility for any opinion or conclusions contained herein. The Federal Government reserves a nonexclusive license to use and reproduce for government purposes, without payment, this material where the government deems it in its interest to do so.

ISBN 0-89818-109-7

Acknowledgments

The following staff and consultants have contributed to the development of this text.

Editorial Directors
Charles N. Quigley
Duane E. Smith
Jane G. Sure

General Editor
Judith A. Matz

Production Directors
Kerin Martin
Theresa Richard

Staff Associates
John Hale
Michael Leong
Gary Mickens
Howard Safier

Consulting Associates
Phyllis Clarke
Gloria Eastman
Tom Fitzgerald
Barbara Miller
Eugenia Moore
David Morgan
Laurel Singleton
John Zola

Typesetters
Roslyn Danberg
Jan Ruyle

Production Assistants
Lise Borja
Anne Drooker
Pat Mathwig
Steve Wasserman

Illustrations and Graphics
Richard Stein

The Center is also grateful for the many helpful comments and suggestions that have been received from the following persons who have reviewed the manuscript in its various developmental stages. The Center has attempted to be responsive to all of the many valuable suggestions for improvement in the text. However, the final product is the responsibility of the Center and does not necessarily reflect the views of those who have contributed their thoughts and ideas.

Margaret Branson, Administrator
Division of Instructional Services
Kern County Public Schools
Kern Country, California

Gary Bryner, Professor
Department of Political Science
Brigham Young University

Maria Cedeno, Teacher
Citrus Grove Middle School
Miami, Florida

Stephen Feinberg
Social Studies Curriculum Leader
Wayland Junior High School
Wayland, Massachusetts

James R. Giese
Executive Director
Social Science Education
 Consortium, Inc.
Boulder, Colorado

Jack N. Hoar, Consultant
Long Beach Unified Schools
Long Beach, California

John LaGore
Magnet Program Specialist
McKinley School
Bakersfield, California

Karen Levine, Teacher
Brooklawn Junior High School
Parsippany Hills, New Jersey

Paula Lieb, Teacher
Churchill Junior High School
East Brunswick, New Jersey

Gary Marksbury
Mentor Teacher/Department Head
Hughes Junior High School
Lakewood, California

Lynn McDonald, Teacher
Groveport, Ohio

Dana Mills, Teacher
Longfellow Junior High
Enid, Oklahoma

Henry Mueller, Coordinator
Middle School Social Studies
Niskayuna Central School District
Niskayuna, New York

Sue Olds
Social Science Department Chair
Holmes Junior High School
Davis, California

Evelyn Richman
Coordinator, Law Program
JHS 166
Brooklyn, New York

Joel Rosen, Teacher
P.S. 99
Brooklyn, New York

Janet Russell
Social Studies Department Head
Shotwell Middle School
Houston, Texas

W.A. "Del" Stelck
Professor Emeritus
Department of History
California State University
Northridge, California

Judy Wolff
Teacher/Department Chair
Mulholland Junior High School
Van Nuys, California

Members of the Commission on the
Bicenntennial of the United States Constitution

Advisory Committee
The Citizen and the Constitution

Board of Directors
Center for Civic Education

Table of Contents

Warren E. Burger, Chairman

Commission on the Bicentennial of the United States Constitution

Chief Justice of the United States, 1969-1986

The years 1987 to 1991 marked the 200th anniversary of the writing, ratification, and implementation of the basic documents of American democracy, the Constitution and the Bill of Rights. Our Constitution has stood the tests and stresses of time, wars and change. Although it was not perfect, as Benjamin Franklin and many others recognized, it has lasted because it was carefully crafted by men who understood the importance of a system of government sufficiently strong to meet the challenges of the day, yet sufficiently flexible to accommodate and adapt to new political,

economic, and social conditions. Many Americans have but a slight understanding of the Constitution, the Bill of Rights, and the later amendments to which we pledge our allegiance. The lessons in this book are designed to give you, the next generation of American citizens, an understanding of the background, creation, and subsequent history of the unique system of government brought into being by our Constitution. At the same time, it will help you understand the principles and ideals that underlie and give meaning to the Constitution, a system of government by those governed.

Preface

This text introduces students to the study of constitutional government in the United States. It is not a text in constitutional law. It is also not a conventional history focusing upon people and events. This book is a history of ideas. It explains the most important ideas of our constitutional system and how they were developed. Its intent is to provide students with an understanding of how the Constitution came into existence, why it took the form it did, and how it has functioned for the past two hundred years.

Since the Founders were acquainted with and influenced by various political philosophies, it is important that students have an understanding of those philosophies if they are to develop an understanding of why the Constitution was written as it was. They must be able to see how the Founders took the ideas of natural rights and republican government and adapted them to the circumstances of America in the eighteenth century. If students are to understand why the Founders believed a written constitution was necessary, they need to know how the Founders understood the idea of constitutional government and where that idea came from.

In addition to political philosophy, history and experience were major influences on the Founders. The text provides students with a description of the major developments in constitutional government in England. It also provides students with an overview of the 150 years prior to the Revolution, during which the colonists had acquired considerable experience in the practice of government.

Students review the reasons why the colonists decided to seek their independence, and examine the Declaration of Independence as a statement of their basic political ideals at the outbreak of the Revolution. Finally, the students learn of the writing of the state constitutions and the Articles of Confederation and how these early constitutions contributed to the development of the view that a new constitution was necessary.

The study of political philosophy and history provides the necessary background for developing an understanding of the writing, adoption, and ratification of the Constitution. The text provides students with information about the major problems that needed to be resolved and the way in which the Framers resolved them. Here it is important for students to learn how the Framers' response to practical problems was shaped by their understanding of history and their commitment to the fundamental principles of natural rights, republicanism, and constitutionalism. A full understanding of the adoption and ratification of the Constitution requires a comprehension of the arguments for and against the Constitution, that is, the arguments of the Federalists and the Anti-Federalists. These arguments must also be understood in the light of the Framers' understanding of political theory and history.

Having studied the writing, adoption, and ratification of the Constitution and developed an understanding of its philosophical foundation, students are now in a position to begin examining the developments of the following two hundred years. The remainder of the text exposes students to a number of controversies, including those over judicial review, federalism, due process, equal protection, and freedom of speech and religion. Students are helped to understand the kinds of arguments that can be made about these issues, the kinds of evidence that are appropriate, and the factors that need to be taken into account in developing informed positions on such issues. One result of this sort of educational experience is that the student is better equipped to participate in contemporary debates on public issues. The ability to participate in this way is one of the most important qualifications of citizenship.

The aim of this text, then, is to provide students with an understanding of the American past and to equip them intellectually to be active participants in the American present and future. It is a text that enables students to learn something about political philosophy, history, and political science. In other words, it attempts to provide students with the foundation of a civic education.

Teaching Methods

This program uses a conceptually oriented approach that blends expository and inquiry methods, both of which call for active student participation. The approach stresses the development of analytic and evaluative skills, which will enable students to apply their knowledge and understanding to a wide variety of political questions and issues. The lesson plans included in this guide suggest a broad range of teaching strategies, including directed discussions, debates, simulations, and small-group problem-solving activities.

This teacher's guide is designed to complement and extend the student text. The lessons usually begin with an optional introductory activity intended to stimulate student interest. These introductory activities are designed to be used prior to the reading of the lesson by the students.

Next is a vocabulary list, labeled "Terms to know." This may be used to pre-teach vocabulary. However, because the text of each lesson typically defines new terms as they are introduced, it may be more appropriate to discuss the vocabulary after the students have read the passage. In that case, the "Terms to know" can be used to check for understanding.

The narrative for each lesson is divided into small segments to make reading manageable for the students. Strategies for presenting and discussing these materials are given in the "Reading and Discussion" sections of the lesson plans. In some lessons, the text introduces the key concepts, which are then reinforced through an activity. In other lessons, the reverse strategy is used. Cooperative learning strategies are suggested in some lessons and would be appropriate in many others.

The lessons include illustrations designed to complement and enhance comprehension of the narrative material. Most of the illustrations lend themselves to small group or interactive teaching strategies. Many of the drawings require students to interpret information, apply facts, theorize, use creative thinking, deductive reasoning, and decision-making skills. Timelines are also included in the introduction to the first five units. They are a useful aid in assisting students to place events in an historical context.

Each lesson in the student text ends with a number of questions entitled "Reviewing and using the lesson." These questions may be used as the basis for concluding the class discussion, for individual student reflection, or for individual or small group homework assignments. Because the text introduces many new concepts, it is especially important for students to have the opportunity to reflect upon what they have just studied.

Keeping a constitutional journal is suggested as an optional learning activity. This activity may be accomplished by giving students four to six minutes at the end of the class period to make entries in their journals on what they have studied and learned. The journal provides an opportunity for students to document what they have learned, to reach new understandings, and to enhance their writing skills. Students may be encouraged to keep their constitutional journals in spiral notebooks so that they can be collected periodically for review and comment by the teacher. We suggest the journals not be graded to avoid inhibiting student candor and creativity.

Students should be introduced to the text by giving them a brief overview of its contents and the activities in which they will be taking part (reading, discussion, individual exercises, and group activities including role playing). Students should understand that this course will introduce them to the basic ideas underlying constitutional government, the way the Founders used these ideas, and the development of constitutional government in this country since the adoption and ratification of the Constitution.

The techniques used in the student text and reinforced in the teacher materials are designed to actively involve the students in the learning process. They are tools to help students understand the American past and their rights and responsibilities as citizens in our constitutional democracy.

Unit One

What is government?

UNIT OVERVIEW

This unit introduces students to the study of the United States Constitution and to the philosophical ideas that provided its foundation. Students first consider some of the basic elements of the natural rights philosophy as it was developed by the English political philosopher John Locke. They are asked to consider some of the important questions about government asked by Locke and others. Why do we need government? What should it do? What makes it legitimate?

Students then examine another important political philosophy that influenced the Founders: republicanism. They learn about the influence of this classical idea on the thinking of the Founders and why they were convinced that this was the best kind of government for Americans.

Students are also introduced to the idea of constitutionalism. The important distinction between constitutional governments and autocratic or dictatorial governments as well as the criteria for making this distinction are described. Finally, they learn two common means of organizing governments to avoid the abuse of power—separation of powers and a system of checks and balances.

UNIT OBJECTIVES

At the conclusion of this unit:

1. Students should be able to explain the following concepts from the natural rights philosophy: natural rights, state of nature, social contract, and the consent of the governed.

2. Students should be able to explain the characteristics of republican government and to discuss the role of civic virtue.

3. Students should be able to distinguish between constitutional governments and autocratic or dictatorial governments.

4. Students should be able to explain separation of powers and checks and balances and how they help prevent the abuse of power.

Why do we need a government?

LESSON OVERVIEW

This lesson introduces the basic concepts of the natural rights philosophy. After being introduced to the concept of natural rights, students are asked to speculate on what might be the benefits and problems of living in a "state of nature," that is, a situation in which there are no laws or government. They compare their ideas about such a situation with those of the English philosopher John Locke. They then learn of Locke's concepts of the social compact and consent, and of the position that the proper purpose of government is the protection of the natural rights of the individual.

LESSON OBJECTIVES

At the conclusion of this lesson:

1. Students should be able to explain the following terms from the natural rights philosophy: natural rights, state of nature, social contract, and consent.

2. Students should be able to explain the problems inherent in a state of nature and their possible solutions, and compare their ideas with those of John Locke.

3. Students should be able to explain how government and laws can protect natural rights.

MATERIALS NEEDED

Student text

TEACHING PROCEDURES

A. Introductory Activity:
Identifying ways to protect rights

Have students read the "Purpose of Lesson" and the "Problem Solving" activity immediately following. Ask students to identify those rights which they think all people should have and list them on the chalkboard. Next, ask students to suggest ways they think these rights can be protected and discuss with them the possible advantages and disadvantages of each means they mention.

B. Reading and Discussion:
Defining concepts of the natural rights philosophy

Have students read the sections entitled "Defining natural rights" and "Protecting natural rights" and discuss with them the terms introduced to be sure they understand and can explain them. Ask them to explain how the illustration relates to the idea of a state of nature. Direct students' attention to the place of John Locke on the timeline at the beginning of the unit and ask them to explain how Americans in the 1780s learned the ideas of an English writer who had lived 100 years before.

C. Problem Solving:
Identifying the problems of a state of nature

Divide the class into groups of 3-5 students and have each group answer the questions in the "Problem Solving" activity. Culminate this activity by having the groups share their responses and discuss them with the entire class.

D. Reading and Discussion:
Comparing students' ideas with those of John Locke

Have students read the remainder of the lesson and compare their lists of the problems of a state of nature with those of John Locke. Be sure students understand the concepts of consent and social compact contained in the final selection.

Direct students' attention to the illustration of the signing of the Mayflower Compact. Ask them to respond to the question in the caption which calls upon them to identify the Mayflower Compact as an example of a social compact.

E. Concluding Activity

Discuss the questions contained in "Reviewing and using the lesson." You may also wish to have students describe the following terms in their own words in their constitutional journals.

> state of nature
> natural rights
> social contract
> consent of the governed
> absolute power

OPTIONAL ACTIVITIES

For Reinforcement, Extended Learning, and Enrichment

1. Ask students to identify examples of behavior in the school and community that illustrate the problems of a state of nature and the advantages of government and rules for protecting individual rights.

2. Have students read about John Locke's life and try to find out if there was anything about his experience that might have contributed to his particular views about human nature and political philosophy.

3. Suggest that students read *Lord of the Flies* and report on how it relates to the concept of a state of nature.

4. Have students write about a right they have, the advantages and disadvantages of the right, and how life would be different if that right were not protected.

What is republican government?

LESSON OVERVIEW

Many of the ideas that influenced the Founders originated in the classical period of the Roman Republic. This lesson provides an opportunity for students to explore the meaning of republicanism and civic virtue as they were said to have been practiced in ancient Rome and to consider how these ideas influenced the thinking and behavior of the Founders.

The lesson opens with a brief description of republican government in Rome and an account of what the Founders thought were the principal characteristics and advantages of republican government. The principal characteristics were the ideas that (1) power is held by the citizens, (2) citizens delegate power to representatives, and (3) the representatives are responsible for promoting the common welfare.

Students also learn of the importance of civic virtue (putting the common welfare above one's selfish interests) to the Founders' beliefs about republican government. This is followed by a selection on the Roman citizen Cincinnatus, a model of civic virtue. The Founders thought the advantages of republican government were that it served the common welfare and promoted freedom and prosperity.

Students then participate in a problem-solving activity which calls upon them to examine the concepts of civic virtue and the common welfare.

The lesson then explains the position taken by the French philosopher Montesquieu that the best way to be sure a republican government serves its proper purposes is to separate its powers and provide for a system of checks and balances.

Finally, students learn about the values of republican government and how they were promoted among the citizenry during the early years of the nation.

LESSON OBJECTIVES

At the conclusion of this lesson:

1. Students should be able to explain why the Founders thought republican government was the best type of government, including the importance of the concepts of the common welfare and civic virtue in a republican government.

2. Students should be able to explain the values of republican government and how they were promoted throughout America.

MATERIALS NEEDED

1. Student text

2. Handout 2-1 (optional)

TEACHING PROCEDURES

A. Reading and Discussion:
Understanding the influence of the
Roman Republic on the Founders

Direct the students' attention to the first illustration in the lesson and inform them that it shows the ruins of a civic building from the Roman Republic that existed in Italy over 2,000 years ago. Have students identify this period on the timeline at the beginning of the unit. Ask them to describe buildings with similar architecture they may have seen in the United States. Then ask them to attempt to answer the question that captions the illustration, "How could a government that existed over 2,000 years ago influence the development of our Constitution?"

Inform the students that they will be reading about life during the Roman Republic and explain that the Founders of our country studied this period of history because they thought the government of the Roman Republic was one of the best governments that had ever existed. Then have students read the "Purpose of Lesson," "The Founders were influenced by their study of history" and "Cincinnatus: a model of civic virtue."

Discuss the sections by asking students:

- What did the Founders believe was the purpose of republican government?
- Can you think of a government leader today who has the characteristics of Cincinnatus?

B. Problem Solving:
Examining civic virtue and the common welfare

Divide the class into groups of 3-5 students and have each group answer the questions in the "Problem Solving" activity. Culminate this activity by having the groups share their responses and discuss them with the entire class.

C. Reading and Discussion:
Understanding how Montesquieu thought a government
should be organized to promote the common welfare

Have the students read the section, "How should a republican government be organized?" Be sure they understand the concepts of the separation of powers, checks and balances, and Montesquieu's position on their importance.

D. Reading and Discussion:
Understanding the values of republican government

Assign the last section, "How were the values of republican government promoted?" Ask students to describe the values of republican government and the ways in which these values were promoted in early American history.

E. Concluding Activity

Discuss the questions contained in "Reviewing and using the lesson."

OPTIONAL ACTIVITIES

For Reinforcement, Extended Learning, and Enrichment

1. Ask students to bring to class excerpts from newspapers or accounts in television programs that raise issues of whether actions of a government serve the common welfare or are "corrupt" (serving special interests at the expense of the common welfare). These examples could be of activities of the U.S. government or the governments of other nations.

2. Invite a representative of local, state, or national government or of a particular interest group that deals with government to speak to the class. Ask the person to provide examples of governmental actions that serve the common welfare and those that serve a special interest at the expense of the common welfare.

3. Have students analyze the excerpts from the *Blue-Back Speller,* Handout 2-1, to identify the personal and civic values it was designed to promote among youth.

Analyzing Evidence

By analyzing primary-source material, we can see how republican values were expressed in American society in our nation's early days. The excerpts below were taken from the *Blue-Back Speller,* a popular reading text of the late 1700s. Look for evidence that the values described in the text were passed on to young people. Write the specific values you see next to the phrases or passages that convey them.

"Lessons of easy words to teach Children to read, and to know their duty."

Lesson 1

No man may put off the law of God;
My joy is in his law all the day.
O may I not go in the way of Sin!
Let me not go in the way of ill men.

Lesson 6

I will not walk with bad men; that I may not be
cast off with them.
I will love the law, and keep it.
I will walk with the just, and do good.

Lesson 12

Be a good child; mind your book; love your school
and strive to learn.
Tell no tales; call no ill names; you must not lie,
nor swear, nor cheat nor steal.
Play not with bad boys; use no ill words at play, spend
your time well, live in peace, and shun all strife.
This is the way to make good men of you, and save
your soul from pain and woe.

Lesson 15

As for those boys and girls that mind not their books,
and love not church and school, but
play with such as tell tales, tell lies, curse, swear, and steal,
they will come to some bad end,
and must be whipped till they mend their ways.

Discuss these questions with members of your class.

1. Do these values reflect the beliefs of the Founders?

2. Is civic virtue for young people the same as it was for the Founders?

3. Do you think these messages contributed to making virtuous citizens?

4. Do the books you read and the television shows you watch encourage you to develop civic virtue?

What is constitutional government?

LESSON OVERVIEW

This lesson helps students understand the concepts of "higher law," "constitution," "constitutional government," and "autocratic or dictatorial government." Students learn that while all nations have constitutions, not all nations have constitutional governments. They then learn the essential characteristics that differentiate constitutional government from autocratic or dictatorial government.

LESSON OBJECTIVES

At the conclusion of this lesson:

1. Students should be able to define "constitution" and "constitutional government."

2. Students should be able to differentiate between constitutional governments and autocratic or dictatorial governments.

3. Students should be able to list the characteristics of the "higher law."

MATERIALS NEEDED

Student text

TEACHING PROCEDURES

A. Introductory Activity:
Developing initial definitions

Write the following words on the chalkboard—"constitution," "constitutional government," and "higher law." Ask the students to write a definition for each. Allow them to consult dictionaries and the glossary contained in the text. Then have students share and discuss their definitions.

B. Reading and Discussion:
Defining "constitution"

Have the students read "Defining constitution." Guide them in a discussion of the definition provided, comparing that definition with those they developed earlier. Help them understand that, according to this definition, every nation has a constitution, whether the government is good or bad.

You may wish to discuss with students the reasons for any discrepancies between their original definitions and the one contained in this text. These might include the fact that "constitution" has a number of meanings. In this text it is being used in the one very specialized meaning that is used in political philosophy, political science, and constitutional law. Dictionary definitions of complex concepts from such fields are often incomplete.

C. Reading and Discussion:
Defining "constitutional government" and "higher law"

Next have students read the sections entitled "Defining 'constitutional government'," and "Defining 'higher law'." Be sure students understand the basic difference between a constitutional government and autocratic or dictatorial governments. Discuss the five characteristics of the higher law in a constitutional government.

Direct students' attention to the illustrations in the lesson and ask them to identify which situation depicted best illustrates a constitutional government and to explain the reasons for their selection. Then discuss the following questions:

What important principles of constitutional government are suggested by the pictures?

What important differences between constitutional and autocratic or dictatorial governments are illustrated?

D. Problem Solving:
Understanding constitutional government

Divide the class into groups of about three to five students and have each group follow the instructions in the "Problem Solving" activity. Culminate this activity by having the groups share their responses and discuss them with the entire class.

E. Concluding Activity

Conclude the lesson by leading a discussion of the questions contained in "Reviewing and using the lesson."

OPTIONAL ACTIVITIES

For Reinforcement, Extended Learning, and Enrichment

1. Assign each student one nation in the world. Each student should find out if the assigned nation has a constitutional government or an autocratic government and explain the reasoning behind their classification.

2. As a constitutional journal activity, you might ask students to write two brief anecdotes. One should be an incident illustrating life under a constitutional government and the other life under an autocratic government.

How can governments be organized to prevent the abuse of power?

LESSON OVERVIEW

This lesson helps students understand that constitutional governments are usually organized in a complex way in order to prevent the possible misuse or abuse of their powers. This organization involves the use of the principles of separation of powers and of checks and balances. Checks and balances means that the powers given to the different branches of government are shared and balanced in such a way that each branch can check the power of the other branches. Students also learn that the complexity of the organization of constitutional governments means it often takes more time to get things done than might be the case with less complicated systems of government. Students learn that this "inefficiency" has been viewed by many people as desirable because it makes it more difficult for governments to misuse power and threaten the rights of the citizens.

LESSON OBJECTIVES

At the conclusion of this lesson:

1. Students should be able to explain the reasons for the separation of powers and for checks and balances in a government.

2. Students should be able to explain the relationship between the separation of powers and the system of checks and balances.

3. Students should be able to describe the three branches of government and explain some of the powers of each.

MATERIALS NEEDED

Student text

TEACHING PROCEDURES

A. Introductory Activity:
Understanding the Founders' fear of the abuse of power

Have students read the "Purpose of Lesson " and the "Problem Solving" sections in the text. Discuss the view of human nature contained in the quotations. Then, either individually or in small groups, have students suggest safeguards they would include if they were writing a constitution in order to prevent the abuse of power. Discuss their suggestions with the entire class. You might conclude this activity by having students write a caption for the first illustration in the lesson based upon their discussion of the Framers' concern with the problem of the abuse of power by government.

B. Reading and Discussion:
Understanding constitutional safeguards

Have students read the remainder of the lesson and compare the safeguards they have developed with those developed by the Framers of the Constitution. Be sure students can explain "separation of powers" and "checks and balances" and give examples of each. Also, be sure students can explain the purposes of these organizational devices and why some people argue that the complexity they engender is beneficial.

C. Concluding Activity

Lead a discussion of the questions in "Reviewing and using the lesson." You may also wish to have students write answers to these questions in their constitutional journals.

OPTIONAL ACTIVITIES
For Reinforcement, Extended Learning, and Enrichment

1. Have students look in newspapers and newsmagazines for examples in current events of one branch of government checking the use of power by another.

2. Have students conduct research and report on noteworthy examples from American history of one branch of the federal government using its constitutional powers to check another branch's power. Instances that you might want to suggest for research are: Roosevelt's plans to enlarge or "pack" the Supreme Court, Watergate, and the Senate hearings on the nomination of Judge Bork to the Supreme Court.

3. Have students research governments of other nations to find out how many employ similar techniques for preventing the abuse of power and what other methods nations use to achieve this goal.

4. Have students select a foreign nation and do research to see if and how it uses the principles of separation of powers, checks, and balances.

Unit Two

What experiences shaped the Founders' thinking about government?

UNIT OVERVIEW

This unit helps students to understand who the Founders and Framers were and what experiences shaped their thinking about government. Students first study the influence on the Framers of their English heritage and their experience with self-government. They learn of the Founders' 150 years of experience with self-government under the British rule of the colonies and why they sought independence. Then they look at the political ideas of the Framers and how these ideas are embodied in the Declaration of Independence. The state constitutions and governments created by the newly-independent states are examined. Next, the students learn about the way of life in the United States in the 1780s. The last lesson sets the stage for the subsequent units by examining why the Founders and Framers believed a new constitution was needed in 1787.

UNIT OBJECTIVES

At the conclusion of this unit:

1. Students should be able to describe British constitutional development through the Magna Carta and the English Bill of Rights, and the influence of that development on the colonial governments.

2. Students should be able to explain in what ways the colonies' governments and ways of life were unique.

3. Students should be able to identify passages of the Declaration of Independence and the state constitutions that embody the natural rights philosophy, republicanism, and constitutionalism.

4. Students should be able to describe some of the characteristics of the state constitutions, the problems that arose under them, and their influence on the Constitution.

5. Students should be able to describe the Articles of Confederation, major accomplishments of the govenment under the Articles, their weaknesses, and explain concerns that led to the Philadelphia Convention.

How were the Americans influenced by their English background?

LESSON OVERVIEW

This lesson traces some important events in the development of English constitutional government. The Magna Carta and the English Bill of Rights, documents often cited but seldom understood, are discussed in terms of their contribution to constitutionalism. Students learn about the social distinctions in English society and how the king's power came to be shared with the nobility and later with the common people. They also learn how this resulted in a shift in the balance of power favoring Parliament. Special emphasis is placed on the concepts of limitations on the monarch's power and representative government.

LESSON OBJECTIVES

At the conclusion of this lesson:

1. Students should be able to explain some of the most important events in the development of English constitutional government.

2. Students should be able to explain how the struggles between the English monarch and Parliament evolved into a system of separated powers and representative government.

3. Students should be able to explain the contributions of such documents as the Magna Carta and the English Bill of Rights to the attitudes of the American colonists toward their government.

MATERIALS NEEDED

Student text

TEACHING PROCEDURES

A. Introductory Discussion:
Reviewing student knowledge

Review with students the idea that most Americans in the 1780s were of English ancestry. Develop their understanding of the Americans' commonality of language, history, religion, and attitudes toward government. Draw out from the class what ideas or facts they have about English government, i.e., king, Parliament, House of Lords, House of Commons. Also review the definition of a constitutional government.

B. Reading and Discussion:
Examining the feudal system

Have students read the "Purpose of Lesson," "Americans' knowledge of British government," and "The feudal system." Be sure students understand the structure of the feudal system and the reasons why the English monarchs came to share power with the nobility. Students may be asked to speculate on how the sharing of power between the king and his nobles eventually led to the growth of constitutional government.

C. Reading and Discussion:
Examining the Magna Carta and its importance

Have the students read "The Magna Carta." Students should learn that the practice of shared powers that had originally developed out of practical necessity grew into a tradition. The nobles came to assume that the tradition was not a privilege but a right. The Magna Carta was a document which emerged from the tradition but which also required a force of arms on the part of the nobles to secure beyond dispute. They should understand that the significance of the Magna Carta in terms of the evolution of constitutional government was its confirmation of the basic ideas of government by contract and limited government. These ideas should be related to their learnings in Unit One.

D. Reading and Discussion:
Reviewing the establishment of Parliament

Have students read "The establishment of Parliament." Have them answer the question posed under the illustration at the bottom of the page about which groups benefited most from the creation of Parliament. Have the students consider which groups were not represented in the new council. Do they think that these groups benefited at all from the establishment of Parliament?

Students should understand that the importance of the establishment of Parliament lies in its embodiment of the idea of representative government and in the subsequent shift in the balance of power from the monarch to Parliament.

E. Reading and Discussion:
Understanding the importance of the English Bill of Rights

Have the students read "The English Bill of Rights." At this point, the students should be able to understand the Bill of Rights as a clear sign of the shift of power away from the monarch.

F. Problem Solving:
Understanding increased protection
of rights in the English government

Have the students divide into groups of three to five to answer the questions posed in the exercise. Then lead students in a discussion of their answers. Ask them why they thought it took over 470 years for the English Bill of Rights to be enacted. To prepare for later discussion of the American Bill of Rights, you may wish to ask students to identify rights they think should be protected that are not included in the text description of the English Bill of Rights. These responses might be recorded to be used when studying the American Bill of Rights.

G. Concluding Activity

Conclude the lesson by leading a discussion of the questions contained in "Reviewing and using the lesson." Emphasize the British origins of many of the basic rights in our Constitution so that students will be prepared to understand the ideas discussed in later lessons.

OPTIONAL ACTIVITIES

For Reinforcement, Extended Learning, and Enrichment

1. Have students research the adoption of the Bill of Rights of 1689. Have groups debate the adoption of the Bill of Rights, with one group representing the king and one the House of Commons.

2. Ask students to imagine they are reporters observing the signing of the Magna Carta at Runnymede in 1215. Have them write a news account for a fictional newspaper in which they describe the scene, what is happening, who the participants are, and what is said. Interviews with leaders and bystanders may be included to get "on the scene" reactions.

3. Students might interview a sample of adults to determine if they know what the Magna Carta and English Bill of Rights said and their significance. Students could follow up the survey with a letter to the editor explaining the result of the survey and what it means regarding adults' perceptions of the importance of these documents.

What experiences led to the American Revolution?

LESSON OVERVIEW

In this lesson students learn about the basic ideas from British constitutional government that were incorporated in American colonial governments--natural rights, higher law, separation of powers, checks and balances, representative government, and the right to vote. The colonists considered themselves to be loyal subjects of England whose initial need for local government was because of the distance that separated them from England. Over time, however, the colonists became accustomed to their own representative governments and considered representative government to be a right — a situation similar to the Magna Carta in which the nobility rebelled against the deprivation of those rights to which they had become accustomed. The students learn of particular events which led to the Revolution, and of the British view in the dispute with the American colonies.

LESSON OBJECTIVES

At the conclusion of the lesson:

1. Students should be able to identify the basic ideas of constitutional government embodied in the American colonial governments.

2. Students should be able to describe British policies and why the colonists began to resist British control.

3. Students should be able to describe American actions which led to armed resistance and the writing of the Declaration of Independence.

NEEDED MATERIALS

Student text

TEACHING PROCEDURES

A. Introductory Activity:
Examining the students' experience with self-government and school governance

Have the students describe what kind of student government exists in their school or other schools they have attended. Ask them to identify any of the basic ideas about government they have studied in such student governments. Then, have students identify in what ways the administration of their school reflects basic ideas of constitutional government.

B. Reading and Discussion:
Identifying basic ideas of constitutionalism in colonial governments

Have the students read the "Purpose of Lesson" and "Constitutional government in the colonies." Write the five basic ideas contained in the text on the board. Discuss how they were used in the colonial governments. Then, have the students speculate on the effects on the colonists of their experiences with self-government over 150 years and what that experience might mean if the British government were to attempt to reduce the rights to which the colonists had become accustomed.

C. Reading and Discussion:
Understanding why the colonists began to resist British intrusion

Have the students read "The British government tightens control over the colonies" and "The colonists begin to resist." Draw the students' attention to the drawings and have them answer the questions in the captions. Have students describe the sequence of events that led to the Revolutionary War.

Ask students to develop the case for the British in their dispute with the Americans. The British point of view is stated briefly in the last paragraph of "The British government tightens control over the colonists." You should also inform students that limited space in the text has precluded an extensive coverage of the Loyalists' and British government's positions on the Revolution. Further, that their positions were not without merit. If time permits, students should be assigned to study these positions and report to the class. This may be tied into the activity described in the "Problem Solving" portion of the lesson.

D. Concluding Activities

Conclude the lesson by leading a discussion of the questions contained in "Reviewing and using the lesson."

OPTIONAL ACTIVITIES

For Reinforcement, Extended Learning, and Enrichment

1. Ask students to research the governmental structure of the Spanish colonies in America. They should look for differences in organization between these colonies and the British colonies. What do these differences reveal about the values of the Spanish and British governments?

2. Have a group of students research the workings of the New England town meeting or the Virginia House of Burgesses and enact a scene for the class based upon one of these governmental bodies.

3. Have students examine the governance of the District of Columbia or the Trust Territories and compare and contrast the status of these governments to those of the colonies.

4. Have students research and report on the positions of the Loyalists and the British government regarding the Revolution. They should also study and report on the experiences of the Loyalists during this period.

What basic ideas about government were in the Declaration of Independence?

LESSON OVERVIEW

This lesson reviews some of the fundamental ideas that influenced the Founders which the students have encountered in earlier lessons—particularly the notions of natural rights, social contract, consent of the governed, and the right to alter or abolish a government that violates its contract with the governed. Students learn how these ideas are reflected in the Declaration of Independence. They also learn how these ideas were used to justify the American Revolution.

LESSON OBJECTIVES

At the conclusion of this lesson:

1. Students should be able to describe the basic ideas about government which are contained in the Declaration of Independence.

2. Students should be able to explain how the Declaration of Independence embodies the concepts of the natural rights philosophy, republicanism, and constitutional government.

3. Students should be able to describe the arguments justifying the separation of the colonies from Great Britain that are found in the Declaration of Independence.

MATERIALS NEEDED

1. Student text

2. Handout 7-1 (optional)

3. Copies of the Universal Declaration of Human Rights (optional)

TEACHING PROCEDURES

A. Introductory Activity:
Examining the wish for independence

Have the students discuss from their own experience or imagine a situation in which they feel the need to be independent. It can be a personal independence from the authority of parents or school, or the independence of a political entity like their city, county, or state from a greater political authority. Investigate the reasons why the students believe independence to be warranted. Are they based upon any of the notions of self-government in which the Founders believed? What drawbacks would there be to such independence? At the teacher's option, the students can then write a paragraph declaring their independence and another paragraph weighing the advantages and disadvantages of doing so. Volunteers might then share their writing with the rest of the class. Encourage the students to revise their own writing the way that Jefferson did—sharing it with others and being willing to compromise and modify their positions.

B. Reading and Discussion:
Becoming acquainted with the authors of the Declaration

Have the students read "Writing the Declaration." Note that, although Jefferson was one of the Founders and later became President, he was not one of the Framers, since he was in Europe on a diplomatic mission in the summer of 1787. Also note the fact that he was not a eloquent orator. Have the students think about the process of writing the Declaration, how a relatively young man was responsible for drafting it and sharing it with only a few colleagues, and then revising it for presentation to the entire Congress. Discuss with them the power of ideas and the power of the pen which this underscores.

C. Reading and Discussion:
Examining the main ideas and basic ideals
of the Declaration

Have the students read "The contents of the Declaration" and "Ideals of the Declaration." Discuss with students the relationship of the Declaration to the natural rights philosophy.

Distribute copies of Handout 7-1 or write the contents of the Handout on the board. Have the students examine the passage from the Declaration or the entire Declaration reproduced in the text for examples of the beliefs listed on the chart.

D. Reading and Discussion:
Understanding the arguments of the Declaration

Have students read, "Arguments of the Declaration" and explain their relationship to the natural rights philosophy.

E. Problem Solving
Understanding the complaints of the Declaration

Have students read, "Complaints against the King" and complete the problem-solving activity that follows this selection in groups of three to five students each.

F. Concluding the Lesson

Conclude the lesson by discussing the questions in "Reviewing and using the lesson."

OPTIONAL ACTIVITIES
For Reinforcement, Extended Learning, and Enrichment

1. Ask the students why the Declaration of Independence might encourage people to form new governments whenever they were dissatisfied with their existing constitution. Ask them what problems this might cause. Have them conduct research to discover the reaction in Great Britain and Europe at the time to the Declaration of Independence. They might also conduct research to find out how the philosophy of the Declaration has influenced contemporary revolutionary movements.

2. In 1948, the United Nations General Assembly adopted a Universal Declaration of Human Rights. Get copies of the Declaration and distribute them to the students. Have them compare it with the Declaration of Independence. Ask them to answer such questions as (1) Does the United Nations Declaration reflect the same basic ideas as the Declaration of Independence? (2) What are the similarities and differences in the two documents? (3) Why do you think that the United States has refused to adopt the Universal Declaration of Human Rights?

3. Have students conduct research on other nations that might have had declarations of independence. Have them read and compare them with the U.S. Declaration of Independence. They should look for examples of the natural rights philosophy, social contract, higher law, right to alter the government, etc. They could investigate to see if the authors of these declarations directly attributed their work to the work of Jefferson.

Analyzing the Declaration of Independence

The Declaration of Independence reflected many of the Founders' beliefs about government. Reread the passage from the Declaration in your text. Find words or phrases that illustrate the ideas listed in the chart below.

Beliefs	Words from Declaration that show beliefs
Natural rights	
Source of natural rights	
Purpose of government	
Social contract	
People's rights to change or do away with the government	

How did the states govern themselves after the Revolution?

LESSON OVERVIEW

One of the major tasks which faced each of the former colonies, after the break with England, was the creation of a new constitution and government for their state. Some wrote new constitutions immediately or simply superficially revised their old colonial charters or constitutions. After the Revolution was over, most took a closer look at their constitutions and rewrote or revised them. In this lesson, the students examine the main features of these state constitutions and are asked to trace the connections between them and the political philosophy that had been common among Americans of the time. Finally, the students examine the Massachusetts constitution and are asked to contrast it with the other 12 state constitutions.

LESSON OBJECTIVES

At the conclusion of the lesson:

1. Students should be able to describe the basic features of the new state constitutions and explain the concept of popular sovereignty.

2. Students should be able to explain the essential differences between the Massachusetts constitution and the other state constitutions.

3. Students should be able to list the arguments for and against legislative supremacy.

4. Students should be able to explain some of the problems that arose under the state constitutions.

MATERIALS NEEDED

1. Student text

2. Handout 8-1 (optional)

TEACHING PROCEDURES

A. Introductory Activity:
Designing a government

Have the students read the "Purpose of Lesson." Then divide the class into small groups. (This exercise can be shortened by dividing the class into seven groups, each assigned to answer one of the major questions of the handout.) Tell the students they are going to participate in an exercise to learn more about the choices the states faced under the Articles of Confederation.

Give each group a copy of Handout 8-1 or write the substance of the Handout on the board. Ask the students to move quickly through the tasks, and set a time limit for the exercise.

Each group is to answer questions about the design of a new government for their former colony. This will involve dealing with basic constitutional issues. At the end of the time period, ask students to explain their decisions and the bases for them.

B. Reading, Discussion, and Problem Solving:
Examining the state constitutions

Have the students read "Writing the state constitutions" and "Basic ideas in the state constitutions." You might write the basic ideas on the board and have the students discuss them.

Next, have students complete the "Problem Solving" activity. This activity is designed to introduce them to the differences between the Massachusetts constitution and those of the other states and to analyze the advantages and disadvantages of the two different systems.

C. Reading and Discussion:
Examining problems of legislative supremacy

Have students read "Legislative Supremacy" and "Legislative supremacy led to serious problems in most states" and discuss the rationale for its use and the problems that arose during this period under the state constitutions. Have them compare their speculations about the advantages and disadvantages of legislative supremacy from the problem-solving exercise with those that occurred.

D. Reading and Discussion:
Identifying differences between the Massachusetts
constitution and those of the other states

Have the students read "The Massachusetts constitution." Help them to understand the differences between Massachusetts and the other states in the way their constitutions were designed to prevent the abuse of governmental power.

D. Concluding Activity

Have the students discuss or write answers to the questions under the heading "Reviewing and using the lesson." You may wish to have students write in their constitutional journals their position on the topic, "Legislative supremacy is the best protection of natural rights."

OPTIONAL ACTIVITIES

For Reinforcement, Extended Learning, and Enrichment

1. Have the students divide into four groups. Assign two of the groups the task of developing arguments in favor of legislative supremacy. Have the other two argue in favor of the form of government created by Massachusetts. Debate the issue "Legislative supremacy is the best protection of natural rights" by having the groups present their arguments. Begin with a group assigned the affirmative side, followed by one assigned the negative side, and alternating thereafter. Allow several minutes for each presentation, then lead a class discussion about which arguments were more convincing and why.

2. Examine the structure of a parliamentary system of government and then compare and contrast it with that of the state governments immediately after the American Revolution.

3. Have students research other state voting requirements of the period and report back during the class study of Lesson 25 on the right to vote.

4. Have the students research and report on the differences in governments around the world which are founded upon similar principles but which govern quite differently.

Creating a State Constitution

1. Describe how your government will be organized.
   - What branches will it have?
   - Which branch of government will be most powerful?
   - What will keep any one branch from becoming too powerful?
   - Will the legislature and the executive be elected separately, or will the legislature select the executive?
   - If there is a judicial system, will the judges be elected or appointed? If appointed, by whom? Will the judges be independent of the legislature and executive?
   - Will the executive be legally allowed to keep secrets from the legislature, or will he or she be required to tell the legislature and the citizens everything?

2. Who will vote for the people who run the government?
   - Will there be a requirement for voters to be of a certain age?
   - How long will the voters have had to be living in the state to be eligible to vote?
   - Will voters have to have some financial stake in the state to be able to vote—like owning a certain amount of property?

3. Will you allow anyone who wants to come into the state to live to do so?
   - What if they do not speak the same language that you do?
   - Will they be required to learn your language if they do not already speak it?

4. Do you want to protect the businesses which already exist in the state from competition with businesses in other states?
   - If so, how will you do it? Will you charge a tax ("tariff") on goods which are brought into the state to be sold?
   - What would you do if a large company in another state which could make shoes more cheaply than local manufacturers charged a price for their shoes that was too low for the local manufacturers to meet—thus forcing the local company to go out of business? Would you try to keep that from happening?

5. What should be done about the Loyalists—those Americans who remained true to the King during the American Revolution?
   - Should they be banished?
   - Should they be allowed to remain in the new state?

6. How should disagreements between states be settled? For instance, if a company in state A is polluting a river which flows into state B—a river which serves as a source of drinking water in state B—should state B be able to stop the company from polluting the water? If there is no national government, how should it do so?

7. How should relations with other countries be handled?
   - If a foreign country has a disagreement with one of the states but no others, should the rest of the states be involved?
   - If a foreign country attacked one of the states but none of the others, should the other states respond?

What were Americans like in the 1780s?

LESSON OVERVIEW

This lesson is designed to help students place the events at the Philadelphia Convention in historical and social context. It does so by giving students a general description of life in the United States in the 1780s. Students learn, for example, that the population was sparse, and that transportation in the vast new nation was difficult. Conditions in America encouraged in the people an attitude of self-sufficiency.

While most people were white English-speaking Protestants, regional, ethnic, and racial diversity did exist. Most free citizens worked hard but had a good standard of living compared to people of other nations of the time. Their advantages included a higher literacy rate than in other countries, which made the spread of information through newspapers and pamphlets possible even into relatively remote communities.

LESSON OBJECTIVES

At the conclusion of this lesson:

1. Students should be able to describe the significant geographic and demographic facts of America of the 1780s.

2. Students should be able to describe the lives of Americans from different regions, races, and social classes in the 1780s.

3. Students should be able to explain the concept of self-sufficiency, and how that attitude affected and reflected Americans' systems of government.

MATERIALS NEEDED

1. Student text

2. Handout 9-1

3. Illustrations showing colonial, revolutionary-era, or early national clothing styles (optional).

TEACHING PROCEDURES

A. Introductory Activity:
Understanding the effects of population sparsity and distances

Have the students estimate how far they live from their neighbors and discuss present means of communication and transportation. Then compare the present circumstances with those during the 1780s. Ask students to speculate upon how the distances between people's homes and the relatively primitive means of communication and transportation during the period might have affected people's lives.

B. Reading and Discussion:
Understanding the land and people

Have the students read the "Purpose of Lesson," the sections on "Geography and population" and "A self-sufficient people." Have the students list the examples of self-sufficiency which they find in the pictures throughout the lesson. Ask them to speculate on how different the lives and attitudes of the Americans of the 1780s are from their own. Ask them to explain why they would or would not like to have lived in America during that time.

C. Reading and Discussion:
Understanding differences and distinctions

Have the students read the sections entitled "Differences in background," "Class differences," and "Limits on opportunities." Have them examine the pictures and answer the questions in the captions. Have them discuss what changes have occurred in the attitudes toward people of different ethnic and racial heritage in America since the Revolution.

D. Reading and Discussion:
Understanding the relationship between self-sufficiency
and attitudes towards government

Have the students read "Attitudes towards government." Ask them if they think that Americans still adhere to an ethic of self-sufficiency. How has that ethic changed over time, if at all?

E. Concluding Activity

Conclude the lesson by discussing the questions in "Reviewing and using the lesson."

Students might be asked to write in their constitutional journals about how self-sufficient they think they are.

OPTIONAL ACTIVITIES

For Reinforcement, Extended Learning, and Enrichment

1. Have students research and report on the status of colonial women. Reports should include information on the legal and political rights of women and their educational opportunities.

2. Ask the students whether or not they think that class distinctions exist in America today. What evidence can they give to support their position? Divide the class into small groups representing different ethnic and racial groups with different incomes and have them report on their perspectives.

3. Present the information from Handout 9-1. Discuss the implications of clothing and grooming styles of the period.

4. Encourage interested students to make detailed maps of the new nation showing, for example, population centers, population density, and transportation routes. Have them contrast maps of the same scale of Europe and America in 1787. Graphs of the 1787 populations of Canada, Mexico, Britain, France, Spain, and the United States may also be prepared and discussed.

5. Ask students to select particular Founders or Framers and research their lives and report on them to the class.

6. Have students research and report on the lives of children in the various colonies.

7. Have students create and analyze maps showing the ethnic diversity of the 13 states and their settlements. They should research and be able to report on such questions as: Why did certain groups settle in certain states? Why did groups settle in certain geographical areas: coastal, tidewater, foothills, mountains, West, South, Northeast?

8. Have the students research and report upon the impact of literacy and abundant newspapers on American attitudes. Have them get a copy of a colonial newspaper and compare and contrast it with the newspapers of today.

9. To help students record what they have learned, make the following constitutional journal assignment:

> Create a character and take his or her role. Based on what you have learned about Americans in the 1780s, select a state of residence, decide on a name, age, and occupation. Decide whether you are a city-dweller or farmer. Also note your ethnic group, religion, style of clothing, food preferences, etc. Assume you are on your way to the Philadelphia Convention. (You might be going as a delegate, spouse, friend, servant, slave, merchant, etc.)

Early American Styles

Colonial Period

The style of clothing worn during the colonial period had its origins in the fashions of the nobility and aristocracy.

Wigs had been popular since the time of Elizabeth I. "Bigwigs" were those who could afford the largest and most expensive wigs. Wigs were usually white or gray to imitate one's much-respected elders. Wigs needed to be powdered and styled by servants.

Knee breeches flattered the mature figure because the calf remained firm, even when the rest of body was aging.

Revolutionary/Constitutional Period

Wigs went out of style but hair was styled and powdered like a wig. Even Quakers styled and powdered their hair.

Fabrics were luxurious; Americans showed off their wealth.

Democratic fashion expressed the attitude that if you could afford it, you could wear it; you didn't need to be an aristocrat to dress well.

Early Republican Period

Both men and women wanted to look young, free, natural. Simpler fabrics were used in an attempt to be part of the common, democratic class of men. Fashions were influenced by French fashion and Napoleon.

Men's hair was short, unpowdered, sometimes greased or curled with an iron. A ribbon, which had held the tail of the wig in a net bag and was tied around the neck, was retained as a neck tie.

Young men, particularly poets, artists, soldiers, were the first to wear long pants.

Why did the Founders
think a new constitution was needed?

LESSON OVERVIEW

In this lesson students learn about the need to organize a national government after the colonies declared their independence from Great Britain. They also learn that the colonists' fears of a strong national government prompted them to create a weak national government under the Articles of Confederation. The lesson describes some of the accomplishments of the new government. It concludes with a description of how the major weaknesses in the national government under the Articles and the fright produced by Shays' Rebellion eventually led to the movement to create a new constitution.

LESSON OBJECTIVES

At the conclusion of this lesson:

1. Students should be able to explain the ideas and events that influenced the writing of the Articles of Confederation.

2. Students should be able to describe the achievements of the country under the Articles of Confederation.

3. Students should be able to describe the problems under the Articles of Confederation and the causes of Shays' Rebellion.

MATERIALS NEEDED

1. Student text

2. Handout 10-1 (optional)

TEACHING PROCEDURES

A. Introductory Activity:
Understanding the concerns of the Framers

Have students read the first two paragraphs in the "Purpose of Lesson." Then ask them to suggest a list of things the colonists might have feared in writing their new constitution. They may identify the fear of a monarch, a powerful but distant national legislature, burdensome taxes, etc. Ask them what effect the way a government is organized has on the way the government runs and the decisions that it makes. Have them identify examples from their own lives, such as the difference it would make if the school principal served at the discretion of the student government rather than the board of education.

B. Reading and Discussion:
Understanding the reasons for creating a weak national government

Have students read the last paragraph of the "Purpose of Lesson" and "The creation of the Articles of Confederation." Ask students why they think the Founders had the two major fears described in this section. Ask them if they think the Articles of Confederation addressed those fears reasonably.

C. Reading and Discussion:
Reviewing the country's successes under the Articles

Have students read "Achievements under the Articles of Confederation." Ask the students how they think that the organization of the government helped the country in the four achievements listed.

D. Reading and Discussion:
Identifying problems of the national
and state governments under the Articles

Have the students read "Problems under the Articles of Confederation" and "Shays' Rebellion." Ask them to speculate whether these problems were caused by the Articles of Confederation alone or by the state constitutions or both. Be sure they understand that a faction is what we would now call an interest group. Help them to understand why factions were thought to violate the basic idea of republicanism.

E. Problem Solving:
Was a new constitution needed?

Divide the class into four groups. Have them complete the problem-solving activity included in the text. Culminate this activity by having the groups discuss their responses with the entire class.

F. Concluding Activities

Have the students read and discuss the questions under "Reviewing and using the lesson."

OPTIONAL ACTIVITIES

For Reinforcement, Extended Learning, or Enrichment

1. Give each student a copy of Handout 10-1 and allow time for students to complete the worksheet. Go over their answers, drawing from the text section entitled "Problems under the Articles of Confederation" to support or amplify material on the worksheet.

2. Have students write essays in which they speculate about what the United States would be like today if the Articles of Confederation had been kept as the constitution.

3. To help students understand the conflict involved in Shays' Rebellion, ask them to imagine that they are taking part in a television interview of the major personalities involved in the rebellion. Assign the roles of TV interviewers to two or three students. Divide the rest of the class into small groups. Each group should represent a historical personality, such as Daniel Shays or one of his followers, and Abigail Adams or other citizens of Massachusetts opposed to the rebellion. Students should research the position of their assigned persons. While they do so, the interviewers should prepare a list of questions focusing on opinions about a stronger national government. After each group prepares a position statement, conduct the simulated television interviews.

4. Provide the students with the following quotes about Shays' Rebellion and ask each to defend the views expressed in the quotation chosen.

   "If they have real grievances, redress them, if possible; or acknowledge the justice of them, and your inability to do it at the moment. If they have not, employ the force of government against them at once." (Washington)

   "I hold it that a little rebellion now and then is a good thing, and as necessary in the political world as storms in the physical. . . . It is medicine necessary for the sound health of government." (Jefferson)

Problems of the Articles of Confederation

From 1781-1789, the government of the new nation was based on a constitution called the Articles of Confederation. The United States was not strong in these years. The written constitution outlining the organization of the government proved to have many faults.

Refer to the following list of provisions of the Articles and to the problems of the Articles of Confederation. Read each provision and place its number beside the problem(s) to which it might have contributed.

The Articles of Confederation

1. Congress was a one-house legislature with its members chosen by the state legislatures. The states paid the salaries of the delegates and could recall them at any time. Each state had one vote.

2. Congress would carry out the laws. When it was not in session, a committee of the states made up of one delegate from each state carried out the functions of the government.

3. State governments carried out the laws passed by Congress.

4. Congress could ask the states for money to fund the government troops to serve in the armed forces.

5. Power to control trade with foreign countries and among states was left to the states.

6. Nine of the thirteen states had to approve of any action or decision of the government.

7. Congress could negotiate with foreign governments and establish its own currency.

8. All the states had to agree before the Articles could be changed.

Problems with the Articles of Confederation:

____1. A man from Massachusetts cannot sell his farm produce in Connecticut.

____2. A family from Virginia traveled to New York. They were unable to buy necessary items because New York merchants refused to accept Virginia currency.

____3. George Martin of Georgia refused to pay debts to loyalist John Dennison of the same state as guaranteed by the Treaty of Paris.

____4. A group of citizens in Virginia imported woolen goods from Great Britain and refused to pay for them.

____5. New Jersey needed funds to conduct the business of the state, so they printed more money.

____6. IOU's in the form of "Continental's" (money owed by the Continental Congress to soldiers of the Revolution) were not paid. South Carolina paid only a portion of its share.

____7. France would not loan money to the new government.

____8. A treaty with Spain was not ratified, although a majority of the states agreed to it.

____9. Congress requested 250 troops from a state by January 1, 1786, but only 125 were sent.

____10. The representatives from the state of Virginia protested that their population was considerably more than Delaware's, but they had the same number of votes in Congress.

Unit Three

What happened at the Philadelphia Convention?

UNIT OVERVIEW

This unit begins by describing the Framers who attended the Philadelphia Convention and how the Convention was organized. Students then explore some of the major conflicts facing the delegates and learn how the Constitution reflects the compromises they reached to resolve those conflicts. The final lessons in the unit discuss the disagreements between the proponents and opponents of the Constitution: the Federalists and the Anti-Federalists. Students learn how these disagreements were related to differing views of the requirements of the natural rights philosophy, republicanism, and constitutionalism.

UNIT OBJECTIVES

At the conclusion of this unit:

1. Students should be able to describe the delegates to the Philadelphia Convention and how the Convention went about its task.

2. Students should be able to describe major agreements and disagreements over the Constitution and how they were resolved.

3. Students should be able to explain the arguments of the Federalists and Anti-Federalists, and how these arguments contained various elements of the political philosophies they have studied.

Who attended the Philadelphia Convention and how was it organized?

LESSON OVERVIEW

This lesson provides students with an understanding of why the Philadelphia Convention was held and the background and characteristics of the fifty-five men who attended it. It also provides students with information on some of the initial decisions made by the delegates and the reasons for them.

LESSON OBJECTIVES

At the conclusion of this lesson:

1. Students should be able to describe the delegates to the convention.

2. Students should be able to describe the agreements made at the start of the Philadelphia Convention.

3. Students should be able to explain why secrecy was considered so important to the successful outcome of the convention.

MATERIALS NEEDED

1. Student text

2. Handout 11-1 (optional)

TEACHING PROCEDURES

A. Introductory Activity:
Suggesting criteria for the selection of delegates

Inform students that the lesson will provide background on the Philadelphia Convention during which our Constitution was written. As an introductory exercise, ask students to imagine that they are planning a convention today to write a constitution for the nation. To help them understand some of the decisions to be made and their implications, have them complete the exercise on Handout 11-1. Then lead them in a critique of the decisions they have made.

B. Reading and Discussion:
Identifying delegates at the convention

Have students read the "Purpose of Lesson" and the first three sections that follow concluding with "Americans who were not at the convention." Then lead a discussion of the common traits of the Framers. You may wish to have the students determine to what degree the delegates met the criteria they thought should be used to select delegates and speculate on the reasons for the differences. Lead students in a discussion of how representative the Framers were of Americans of their time and whether they think such a group would develop a constitution that would protect the rights of all Americans.

C. Reading and Discussion:
Understanding initial decisions of the Framers

Have students read, "The convention begins" and discuss whether they think the Framers' decision to ignore their instructions from Congress was justified. Then discuss the Framers' reasons for keeping the proceedings of the convention secret and whether the students think this decision was justified. Students should review, with your help, the basic ideas about government which the Framers shared despite differences about detail.

D. Concluding Activity

Conclude the lesson with a discussion of the questions contained in "Reviewing and using the lesson." You may also wish to assign students the task of including their answers to one or more of these questions in their constitutional journals.

OPTIONAL ACTIVITIES

For Reinforcement, Extended Learning, and Enrichment

1. Ask students to locate information about "sunshine laws" or "executive sessions." "Sunshine laws" require governmental bodies to hold open meetings when public policies are being discussed or political decisions are being made. "Executive sessions" of governmental agencies are closed to the public. Students should discuss the advantages and disadvantages of such practices and relate their findings to the decision to keep the constitutional debates secret.

2. Frame one or more of the issues described in the lesson as a debate question. Have students select those in which they are interested and prepare arguments or panel discussions on the topics.

3. Have various students research the backgrounds of the Framers and write brief descriptions of each Framer. Ask them to report on any similarities and differences in the group.

Constitutional Conventions: Then and Now

Using your text, complete the column that asks for information about the Philadelphia Convention of 1787. The second column asks for decisions regarding a modern constitutional convention. Complete this column by discussing the questions with a parent, teacher, neighbor, or other adult. Be prepared to explain your answers.

Issue	Then: 1787	Now: 19??
1. Should a convention be called to "fix" the central government? Explain.		
2. Where is the convention to be held? Why?		
3. Who will lead the convention? Why would you choose this individual?		
4. Should the discussions during the convention be kept secret? Why or why not?		
5. What are the characteristics of the delegates? (age, occupation, income, past experience, etc.)		
6. What specific groups in society do the delegates to the convention represent?		
7. How many delegates will attend the convention?		
8. For what purpose is the convention being called?		

What was the conflict over representation?

LESSON OVERVIEW

Although the Framers agreed on a number of matters, they also disagreed on some important issues. The next three lessons introduce students to the major conflicts that faced the delegates and how they were resolved. These conflicts were over representation of the states in Congress, economic differences between the North and the South, and the issue of how much power should be given to the national government. This lesson focuses on the conflict over representation in Congress and the compromise reached to resolve that conflict.

The lesson opens with a reading on the debate between the states with smaller and larger populations. It is followed by a problem-solving activity where students simulate the convention committee that was assigned to develop a solution on the issue of representation. Next, the students read about the provisions of the Great Compromise arrived at by the Framers to deal with this issue.

LESSON OBJECTIVES

At the conclusion of this lesson:

1. Students should be able to explain why representation was an issue at the convention and the opposing groups and their positions.

2. Students should be able to explain the concepts of equal and proportional representation.

3. Students should be able to describe the key features of the Great Compromise.

MATERIALS NEEDED

Student text

TEACHING PROCEDURES

A. Introductory Activity:
Identifying the problem of representation

Ask students to imagine that they are delegates to the convention and they have to decide how many representatives each state should be able to send to Congress. Lead them in a discussion focusing upon what problems they might encounter in making such a decision. Ask them why the number of representatives a state could send to Congress would be of concern to the delegates and how this concern might be related to the interests of the various states.

You may want to list the problems students identify on the chalkboard so they can compare them with the problems debated by the Framers.

B. Reading and Discussion:
Understanding the conflict over equal and proportional representation

Have students read the "Purpose of Lesson" and the section entitled "The conflict between the large and small states." Compare the problems students identified during the Introductory Activity with those presented in the reading. Then refer students to the description of the differences between larger and smaller populated states in their text and ask these questions to check for understanding.

- Which states do you think probably favored equal representation? Why?

- Which states probably favored proportional representation? Why?

- Virginia and Massachusetts took the same position on this issue, though they were quite different in many ways. Why?

C. Problem Solving:
Developing proposed solutions to the problem of representation

Follow the directions in the student text to conduct this activity. Tell students this exercise asks them to do exactly what the Framers did at the convention: form a committee of delegates from small and large states to develop a solution to the problem of representation to present to the entire convention.

D. Reading and Discussion:
Comparing solutions with the Framers' solution

Have students read "The Great Compromise" and compare and discuss their solution with the solution reached by the Framers.

E. Concluding Activity

Conclude the lesson with a discussion of the questions provided in "Reviewing and using the lesson." You may also wish to ask students to write in their constitutional journals what position they would have taken at the convention on the issue of representation.

OPTIONAL ACTIVITIES

For Reinforcement, Extended Learning, and Enrichment

1. Remind students that they learned earlier that James Madison had come to the convention with a written proposal, called the Virginia Plan. Have students research the Virginia Plan to determine what Madison's views were on the issue of representation discussed in the lesson.

2. Have students gather census data from several different periods in U.S. history. Ask them to compare how Congress would have been constituted if a strict system of equal or proportional representation had been used. What states would have benefitted at various stages in history? What states would have lost impact?

   Note: This question is especially interesting in relation to the pre-Civil War years, when new states were admitted in pairs to keep the balance between free and slave states. (The Census Bureau has a large wall map showing apportionment in the 1st, 25th, 50th, 75th, and 100th Congresses, which would be very useful in this activity.)

3. Have students gather current census data and speculate which states might today favor equal representation and which might favor proportional representation. Then have them speculate on whether they think any of the original 13 states would take different positions today than they did at the convention. Why or why not?

What were the conflicts between the northern and southern states?

LESSON OVERVIEW

By the time of the convention, the differing economies of the northern and southern states had resulted in conflicting economic and political interests. This lesson looks at the conflict at the convention between the northern and southern states over the issues of protective tariffs and slavery.

Students will first read about the differing economies of the North and the South and how these contrasting economic backgrounds led to conflicting views on slavery and tariffs.

Then students participate in a problem-solving activity where they play the role of the committee members who were assigned to settle the disputes between the two regions. Finally, the students compare their resolutions of the problem with the compromises made by the Framers.

LESSON OBJECTIVES

At the conclusion of this lesson:

1. Students should be able to explain the economic basis for differences between North and South.

2. Students should be able to explain the differing views on protective tariffs and slavery between the North and the South.

3. Students should be able to explain the "three-fifths clause" and the "fugitive slave clause" and identify what issues they were intended to resolve.

MATERIALS NEEDED

Student text

TEACHING PROCEDURES

A. Introductory Activity:
Identifying possible sources of conflict

Write the two headings "Northern States" and "Southern States" on the chalkboard and have students provide whatever information they may have about each at the time of the convention. List their comments under the appropriate heading. Then ask them to speculate on whether any of the information they have noted might have led to conflicts between the delegates to the convention from the northern and southern states.

B. Reading and Discussion:
Understanding the conflict between the interests
of the North and the South

Have students read the "Purpose of Lesson" and the sections entitled "The conflict between the northern and southern states," "The conflict over protective tariffs," and "The conflict over slavery." Duplicate the headings on the board from the above activity. Then ask students to recall the characteristics of the northern and southern states they have just read and record them under the proper heading. Ask students to explain the conflicts between the North and the South and their bases. Then, have students compare what they have read with their earlier speculation.

C. Problem Solving:
Developing proposed solutions to the problems

Inform students that the problem-solving activity requires them to deal with the conflicts they have been studying in the same way the Framers did, by referring the problem to a committee to develop a solution. Then divide the class into groups and have them follow the directions noted in the student text.

After the groups have presented their proposed solutions, you might ask some questions that will clarify the process of compromise. For example, you might ask:

- What was the biggest difference of opinion in your group?
- How did you get the people holding different views to agree upon a solution?
- What, if anything, did some members give up in order to get something they wanted?
- Did anyone get everything he or she wanted? How?

D. Reading and Discussion:
Comparing solutions with the Framers' solutions

Have the students read the section on "Compromises made to get southern states to sign the Constitution." Be sure they can explain what the northern and southern states gave up and what they got in return in reaching the compromises. They should understand the purpose of the compromises, and how the compromises are reflected in the Constitution.

Finally, refer students to the table of the slave populations of the states and lead them in a discussion helping them to understand the importance of the "three-fifths clause" to the South.

E. Concluding Activity

Conclude the lesson by leading a discussion of the questions contained in "Reviewing and using the lesson." As a constitutional journal activity, have students describe a compromise they have reached in their own lives and compare the process of compromise in their personal experiences with the process at the convention.

OPTIONAL ACTIVITIES

For Reinforcement, Extended Learning, and Enrichment

1. Divide the class into three groups. Two of these groups should prepare for and debate opposing positions on the following question: Resolved: "The delegates to the Philadelphia Convention were wrong to compromise on the issue of slavery." The third group should listen to the debate, question the opposing teams, render a decision on the issue, and explain its reasoning.

2. Students may be asked to go to a library and find some of the Framers' speeches on slavery. George Mason's is of particular interest.

What was the conflict over the legislative power of the national government?

LESSON OVERVIEW

Despite the fact that the Framers had agreed on creating a stronger national government, there was no consensus on the amount of power that should be granted to the central government. This lesson examines the debate over what should be the scope and limits of the powers of the new Congress.

Students first examine the concerns of the Framers over the scope of power for the Congress and review the compromises over representation that alleviated this concern to some degree. They then learn of the dispute over using general or specific language in the Constitution to delegate power to the Congress. The advantages and disadvantages of general and specific language are explored as is the solution of the Framers which involved using both. Students learn that the general language of Article I, the "necessary and proper" and "general welfare" clauses, have enabled the federal government to increase its power far more than anticipated by the Framers.

LESSON OBJECTIVES

1. Students should be able to explain the experiences that shaped the Framers' views on how much power the national government should have.

2. Students should be able to explain the arguments in the debates over congressional power and to describe how they affected the way the Constitution was written.

3. Students should be able to explain the reasons for specifically enumerating the powers of Congress, for including the necessary and proper and general welfare clauses, and the apparent contradiction between the approaches.

MATERIALS NEEDED

1. Student text

2. Handout 14-1 (optional)

TEACHING PROCEDURES

A. Introductory Activity:
Reviewing the need for a stronger national government

Review with students the weaknesses of Congress under the Articles of Confederation and the reasons why the Founders had created such a weak national government. Then discuss with them why the delegates at the convention wanted to create a stronger national government and ask students to speculate on what fears the Framers might have had about doing so. Finally, ask students to suggest ways the Constitution could be written to give enough power to the national government to fulfill its responsibilities, but not so much power that it could be abused.

B. Reading and Discussion:
Understanding the problem of limiting power

Have students read the "Purpose of Lesson." Then have students read the sections on "How much power should be given to Congress?" Review with the students the concerns of the various delegates over the power of the national government.

C. Reading and Discussion:
Understanding the problem of broad and narrow language

Have students read, "How should the Constitution be written to give power to Congress?" An understanding of this problem is important for understanding later lessons. Be sure students understand the advantages and disadvantages of writing constitutional limitations on power in general and in specific language. (To simplify matters, we have used the terms "general" and "specific" language to refer to what scholars commonly refer to as "broad" and "narrow" language when referring to particular phrases of the Constitution—for example, the specifically enumerated powers of Article 1, Section 8 such as the power to "lay and collect taxes" and the more general "elastic clauses" such as the "necessary and proper" and "general welfare" clauses.

D. Reading and Discussion:
Understanding the Framers' solution

Have students read the section "Specific powers of Congress," "General powers of Congress," and "A source of conflict." Discuss the solution with the students and ask them if they can predict any problems that might have arisen after the convention because of the Framers' use of both specific and general language in attempting to limit the powers of Congress while still giving it enough power to fulfill its responsibility. Any potential problems they identify may be recorded in their constitutional journals to review in the light of future lessons.

E. Problem Solving
Understanding potential problems of language in the Constitution

Have students complete the problem-solving activity and discuss their responses to the questions it contains.

F. Reading and Discussion:
Understanding a source of conflict

Have students read, "A source of conflict" and "What does Article I do?" Discuss the content of these sections with them in preparation for subsequent lessons which will amplify their understanding of the issues it raises.

G. Concluding Activity

Discuss with the students their answers to the questions under "Reviewing and using the lesson."

OPTIONAL ACTIVITIES

For Reinforcement, Extended Learning, and Enrichment

1. Have students conduct research to determine political conflicts that have arisen during U.S. history over the meaning of the "necessary and proper" clause.

2. Have students review the limitations placed upon state governments in Article I, section 10 and write explanations of the advantages and disadvantages of one or more of the limitations.

3. Have students collect articles from newspapers about Congress to develop a bulletin board on the institution.

4. Have students complete Handout 14-1.

Congressional Powers

Directions: Using the Constitution as a reference, decide if the following are examples of the use of Congressional power under specific (mark with an "S") or general ("G") language of the Constitution. If the example is not a power of Congress, place an "X" in the blank. Be prepared to give evidence to support your answers.

_____ 1.   Congress refuses to provide money to aid rebels in Central America.

_____ 2.   Congress raises the tariff on goods imported from Japan.

_____ 3.   A tax reform bill is passed.

_____ 4.   Soldiers are sent to the Middle East.

_____ 5.   No candidate gets a majority of the electoral votes. The House elects a President.

_____ 6.   The Senate rejects the nomination of a Supreme Court justice.

_____ 7.   Congress votes to add two more seats to the Supreme Court.

_____ 8.   Congress authorizes the minting of a silver dollar.

_____ 9.   The House holds hearings on the problem of AIDS.

_____ 10.   A tax is placed on items sold to China.

_____ 11.   The defense budget is cut by several billion dollars.

_____ 12.   A treaty negotiated by the President is approved by the Senate.

_____ 13.   A Veterans Department is created to advise the President.

_____ 14.   Congress appoints a new Secretary of Defense.

_____ 15.   The House authorizes money for a new bomber.

How much power should be given to the executive and judicial branches?

LESSON OVERVIEW

After deciding upon the powers of Congress to be included in Article I of the Constitution, the Framers turned to the task of deciding upon the proper scope and limits of power for the executive and judicial branches. Students read of the Framers' fears of creating too strong an executive branch and the resulting provisions for checks and balances they include in the Constitution. They also read of the issues raised concerning the method of selecting the President and the development of the electoral college. The lesson concludes with an examination of the federal judiciary.

LESSON OBJECTIVES

At the conclusion of this lesson:

1. Students should be able to explain the basic organization of the executive and judicial branches.

2. Students should be able to explain why the Framers created the electoral college as the method for selecting the President.

3. Students should be able to explain the role of the federal judiciary.

MATERIALS NEEDED

Student text

TEACHING PROCEDURES

A. Reading and Discussion:
Understanding the Framers' design of the executive branch

Have the students read the "Purpose of Lesson," and the first three sections on "How much power should be given to the executive branch?" "The Framers' solution," and "How should the President be selected?" Be sure students understand the various ways the Constitution provides for checks upon the powers of the Presidency, the reasons for these provisions, and the reasons for the Framers' creation of the electoral college.

B. Reading and Discussion:
Understanding the Framers' design of the judicial branch

Have the students read and then discuss the section on "How much power should be given to the judicial branch?" Be sure that they understand the distinction between original jurisdiction and appellate jurisdiction and the meaning of the supremacy clause.

C. Reading and Discussion:
Understanding basic differences in the new national government

Have students read the section on "The new national government." It is important that the students understand that the new national government differed from the government under the Articles of Confederation—it could act directly on the people. Discuss with them the concept of enumerated powers and the supremacy of the Constitution and federal laws over the state constitutions and state laws.

D. Concluding Activity

Discuss with the students their answers to the questions under "Reviewing and using the lesson." You may wish to have students record their answers in their constitutional journals.

OPTIONAL ACTIVITIES

For Reinforcement, Extended Learning, and Enrichment

1. Have students research some of the alternatives to the electoral college that have been debated, along with suggested alternatives to the present term of office. They should identify the advantages and disadvantages of each alternative.

2. Have students collect newspaper clippings that demonstrate different powers and duties of the President or the Supreme Court.

What opinions did the Framers have of the Constitution?

LESSON OVERVIEW

In this lesson students learn of some of the disagreements about the Constitution that set the stage for the debates over its ratification. These are significant because many have to do with issues that are still discussed and debated today. Students read a summary of a statement by Benjamin Franklin, who supported the adoption of the Constitution, as well as the objections of George Mason, who opposed it. Student analysis of the objections of George Mason focuses upon his use of the basic ideas of constitutional government, republicanism, and representative government to make his case against the Constitution.

LESSON OBJECTIVES

At the conclusion of this lesson:

1. Students should be able to explain Benjamin Franklin's reasons for favoring the adoption of the Constitution.

2. Students should be able to explain the criticisms of George Mason, give examples of historical events that illustrate them, and explain constitutional provisions designed to deal with them.

MATERIALS NEEDED

Student text

TEACHING PROCEDURES

A. Introductory Activity

Have the students describe political debates they have heard. Ask them if they have ever agreed with some of the arguments on both sides of the debate. Ask them how they reconciled those arguments and came to conclusions.

B. Reading and Discussion: Understanding Franklin's position

Have students read the "Purpose of Lesson" and "Franklin urges acceptance of the Constitution." Help them to understand the doubts Franklin appears to have had and his reasons for supporting the Constitution despite them.

C. Reading and Problem Solving: Understanding George Mason's position

Have students read "George Mason's objections to the Constitution." Then divide the class into seven groups and follow the instructions contained in the "Problem Solving" activity.

After the group work and class discussion of its results, note the importance of Mason's criticism of the Constitution for its lack of a bill of rights.

D. Concluding Activity

Conclude the lesson by leading a discussion of the questions included in "Reviewing and using the lesson." You may ask students to record their responses in the constitutional journals.

OPTIONAL ACTIVITIES

For Reinforcement, Extended Learning, and Enrichment

1. Ask the students to write a paragraph in their constitutional journals speculating on what would have happened if the Constitution had not been ratified.

2. Select students to read from a biography of John Hancock of Massachusetts and report to the class how he was persuaded to support the Constitution.

3. Have students work in pairs or in small groups to complete the following exercise.

    Ask students to turn to the section "George Mason's objections to the Constitution" in the lesson. Ask them to reread each of George Mason's objections and identify for each objection the principle of government Mason believed the Constitution may have violated. Discuss their ideas as a class.

4. Have students read about the life of Virginia governor Edmund Randolph, to explore why he first supported the Constitution, then opposed it, and finally supported it at the Virginia state ratification convention.

Who were the supporters and critics of the Constitution?

LESSON OVERVIEW

In this lesson, students learn about the arguments the Federalists and Anti-Federalists used in the ratification debates. The Anti-Federalists' criticisms of the Constitution were based on traditional ideas about the requirements for republican government. These ideas included the need for a small community of citizens of similar means and interests, who possessed civic virtue, and were dedicated to the common welfare.

Students learn that the Federalists argued that it was unrealistic, in an extended republic, to rely upon the traditional notion of a small nation of citizens possessing civic virtue. Instead, the Federalists argued that protection of natural rights and promotion of the common welfare could be achieved through a federal system consisting of complex provisions for representation, separation of powers, and checks and balances.

Students read about the ratification strategy that was used by the Federalists, and then in small groups discuss the arguments of the Federalists and Anti-Federalists.

LESSON OBJECTIVES

At the conclusion of this lesson:

1. Students should be able to explain why the Federalists wanted the Constitution to be ratified in state conventions and the arguments they used to justify this procedure.

2. Students should be able to explain the arguments made by the Federalists in support of the Constitution. They should be able to explain how the arguments differed from traditional views of republican government.

3. Students should be able to explain the arguments of the Anti-Federalists and how those arguments were based upon traditional ideas of republican government.

4. Students should be able to explain how the debate between the Federalists and Anti-Federalists led to the development and adoption of the Bill of Rights.

MATERIALS NEEDED

Student text

TEACHING PROCEDURES

A. Introductory Activity:
Developing a ratification strategy

Have the students read the "Purpose of Lesson." Then divide the class into groups of three to five students and have them read and discuss the opening section, "What happened after the Philadelphia Convention?" Ask each group to think of at least one strategy they would use to gain acceptance of the new Constitution. Allow groups to describe briefly the strategies they have developed.

B. Reading and Discussion:
Understanding the Framers' strategy

Have students read "The Framers ask the voters to approve the Constitution." Discuss how the Federalists' plan was similar to or different from the student-developed plans. Help students understand how the Framers used the concept of the social compact in the ratification of the Constitution.

C. Reading and Group Activity:
Understanding the Federalists' and Anti-Federalists' positions

Have students read the sections "The struggle for ratification" and "Arguments for and against the Constitution." Organize the class into three groups. Then use the following procedure.

- Group A should read and discuss the first two sets of positions of the Anti-Federalists and Federalists.
- Group B should read the second two sets of positions.
- Group C should read the third two sets of positions.

After the groups have had sufficient time to study and discuss the positions, have representatives of each group explain the positions it has studied to the rest of the class. After each group has completed its presentation, the class should discuss whether the Federalist or Anti-Federalist positions are most convincing on each topic.

D. Reading and Discussion:
Understanding the reasons for the Bill of Rights

Have the students read the last section, "The agreement to add a bill of rights." Stimulate discussion with the following questions:

- Do you agree with the Federalists or the Anti-Federalists on the issue of a bill of rights? Why?
- Why do you think the Anti-Federalists were able to win this concession from the Federalists?

E. Concluding Activity.

Conclude the lesson by conducting a class discussion of the questions in "Reviewing and using the lesson." Students might be asked to write a summary paragraph in their constitutional journals indicating whether they would have voted for or against ratification had they had the opportunity to vote in 1787.

OPTIONAL ACTIVITIES

For Reinforcement, Extended Learning, and Enrichment

1. Have students study the ratification battle in New York in detail. They should prepare reports on the battle; the conclusion should state why the Federalists were successful there.

2. Have students conduct research on George Mason, Mercy Otis Warren, and other prominent Anti-Federalists. They should present their findings to the rest of the class.

3. Have the class conduct a ratification debate between the Federalists and the Anti-Federalists as the final activity of this unit. You may wish to have this held before a panel of judges selected from the community. The activity would probably require two days to complete. Use the following procedures for the debate.

a. Divide the class into two teams. Assign one team the task of developing a ten-minute presentation on the arguments of the Federalists. Assign the other team the task of developing a similar presentation on the arguments of the Anti-Federalists.

b. Divide each team into groups consisting of five students each. Ask these smaller groups to do research to identify arguments and supporting information on their team's position. The small groups may be assigned different research tasks. Reference materials may include copies of the arguments set forth by the Federalists and Anti-Federalists located in the Reference Section of this teacher's guide, the information contained in Lesson 17 of the text, or other reference materials you identify.

c. After they have completed their research, the groups composing each team should work together to develop the sequence of points to be made in presenting the team's position.

d. Each team should then select from three to five students to present its position before the class. After the presenters have been selected, they should rehearse their arguments before the rest of the members of their team who, acting as judges, should question the presenters during and after their presentations.

e. Start the hearing by having the spokespersons for the Federalist position present their arguments orally, taking about ten minutes. Questions should be asked only after the presentation is completed. This same procedure should be used for the Anti-Federalists' team.

Unit Four

How was the Constitution used to establish our government?

UNIT OVERVIEW

This unit describes how the Constitution set forth the basic organization of our system of government and some of the more important developments under the new Constitution. Students first learn what a federal system is and how the Constitution established a federal system based on popular sovereignty. They learn how the executive and judicial branches were organized under the Constitution and how the Bill of Rights was added to the Constitution. The text then discusses a development the Framers had not anticipated: the rise of political parties. Students learn why this was significant from the point of view of both the Framers' expectations and for American politics. Finally, students learn about the development of and controversies over judicial review.

UNIT OBJECTIVES

At the conclusion of this unit:

1. Students should be able to explain the basic elements of our federal system, its basis in popular sovereignty, and some of the common problems arising from such a system.

2. Students should be able to describe how the executive and judicial branches were organized.

3. Students should be able to explain how and why the Bill of Rights was added to the Constitution.

4. Students should be able to describe why the development of political parties was important.

5. Students should be able to define judicial review, explain how it developed, and describe some of the disputes that arose about it.

What was the federal system created by the Constitution?

LESSON OVERVIEW

This lesson is intended to help students understand the federal system of government created by the Framers. They learn that the Preamble to the Constitution makes it clear that, under our system of government, sovereignty belongs to the people and that the people delegate power to both federal and state governments and retain some powers for themselves. This federal system is contrasted with unitary and confederate systems. Students also learn that the supremacy clause of the Constitution makes it clear that in the inevitable conflicts between the federal and state governments, the authority of the Constitution is superior to the power of the states.

LESSON OBJECTIVES

At the conclusion of this lesson:

1. Students should be able to describe our federal system, the source of its powers, and how powers are distributed within it.

2. Students should be able to explain the essential differences between unitary, confederate, and federal systems of government.

3. Students should be able to explain some of the factors that have contributed to the growth of the national government.

4. Students should be able to explain how the Constitution gives the federal government supreme power over the state governments.

MATERIALS NEEDED

1. Student text

2. Handouts 18-1, 18-2 (optional)

TEACHING PROCEDURES

A. Introductory Activity:
Reviewing the issue of the distribution of power

Introduce the lesson by explaining that the class will be looking at how power was to be distributed between the new federal government and the state governments. Remind students that most of the Framers, while wanting to create a more powerful federal government, were still suspicious of making that government too powerful at the expense of the state governments.

B. Reading and Discussion:
Defining unitary, confederate, and federal government

Have students read the first two sections, "The Purpose of Lesson," and "Different kinds of government." To help students understand the different kinds of government, have them complete the "Problem Solving" activity. They should then read the section "A new kind of government." Be sure students understand and can explain the concepts of sovereignty and that of federal, unitary, and confederate systems of government. Ask them to give examples of each type of system if they can, e.g., the present United States is a federal system, under the Articles of Confederation we were a confederate system, and Great Britain is a unitary system.

C. Reading and Discussion:
Understanding federalism

Have students read the next two sections, "The distribution of power in the federal system" and "The supremacy of the federal government." Be sure they understand that the people are the ultimate source of power in our system and that in the Constitution they have delegated some power to the state and federal governments and retained some powers for themselves. Also, be sure they understand that the supremacy clause of the Constitution places the federal government in a position of superior power over state governments.

D. Reading and Discussion:
Understanding the complexity of the federal system and sources of conflicts

Have students read the last section, "Conflicts between federal and state governments." Discuss with them how the complexity of the federal system was thought by the Framers to be an advantage.

E. Concluding Activity

Conclude the lesson with a discussion of the questions in "Reviewing and using the lesson." You may wish to have students enter their answers to one or more of these questions in their constitutional journals.

OPTIONAL ACTIVITIES

For Reinforcement, Extended Learning, and Enrichment

1. This lesson states that most laws that affect us directly are state laws. Have students keep track of their actions and activities for one school day. How were their actions or activities affected by laws? How many are federal laws? State laws? City or county ordinances?

2. Have students check newspapers for examples of issues that illustrate controversies over the division of power between the state and federal governments. Have them make a bulletin board of articles illustrating these issues.

3. Divide the class into groups of three to five students each. Distribute Handouts 18-1 or 18-2 to each group. Ask students to read the handouts and follow the instructions they contain. When they have concluded their discussions, ask each group to report its decision to the class and to explain its position.

Drunken Driving and the Nation

The issue of the relationship between the power of the federal and state governments is still alive today. An example is the problem of controlling drunk driving. Thousands of people are killed or injured each year by drunk drivers. Traditionally, each state government has dealt with this problem in its own way, and the federal government has done very little to interfere with the laws they have passed. However, recent complaints about this problem and claims that some states have not done enough to solve it have led to the federal government passing laws to attempt to deal with it. Take the following situation as an example.

When the voting age was lowered to 18 years old in 1972, many states also lowered the age of adulthood, including the right to drink alcoholic beverages. This has resulted in a dramatic increase in alcohol-related deaths in the age group of 18-21 year olds. Despite the fact that allowing 18-21 year olds the right to drink clearly increases highway deaths, a number of states have not raised the legal age at which people can drink.

To deal with this problem, the federal government passed a law that would withhold federal highway construction money from states that did not raise the legal drinking age to 21 by a certain date. The sums of money involved were very large and were needed by the states to build new highways and to keep their present highways in safe condition.

1. Explain the advantages and disadvantages of giving either the state or the federal government the power to determine the legal age for drinking alcoholic beverages.

2. Explain why you would support or oppose the action taken by the federal government.

3. What benefits would the nation receive from a uniform drinking age in all states?

4. What costs would the nation incur from a uniform drinking age in all states?

5. Take and defend a position on this issue.

Highway Safety

Highway safety groups have wanted Congress to pass a law requiring that new cars have a device that would automatically protect the front-seat occupants from injury in head-on collisions; these devices are called "passive restraints." The car manufacturers have come up with two devices: the air bag and the automatic seat belt. Either device would automatically protect the drivers who refuse or were too lazy to buckle their seat belts. These devices are expensive and would add at least $500 to the price of a new car. Most car manufacturers opposed the proposed new requirements. Few new car buyers chose to purchase passive restraint devices, when offered as optional equipment.

1. Should drivers be forced to buy such devices for their cars?

2. What level of government should require these devices — state or federal?

3. What are the advantages and disadvantages of one level of government enforcing traffic and vehicle safety laws over another?

4. What should Congress do? Why?

Many people argue that air bags give drivers and passengers the most protection. Congress finally passed a law requiring the installation of the air bags in all new cars. However, the law was written so air bags would not be required if two conditions were met by state governments:

(a) New state laws would have to be passed requiring the fastening of seat belts while riding or driving in a car.

(b) These new seat belt laws would have to be passed in enough states to encompass over fifty percent of the population.

The required number of states passed such laws and the air bag requirement did not go into effect.

1. Take and defend a position on whether this action by Congress, which required state governments to comply with the law it passed, was justified.

2. Take and defend a position on whether this problem should be dealt with by federal or state governments.

How was the new government established?

LESSON OVERVIEW

This lesson explains how the first President and the first Congress filled in the details of the new government for which the Constitution provided a framework. Other important accomplishments of the first Congress were the passage of the Judiciary Act of 1789 which created the federal court system, and the drafting of the Bill of Rights which was ratified in 1791.

LESSON OBJECTIVES

At the conclusion of this lesson:

1. Students should be able to explain that the Constitution provides a general framework outlining how the government should be organized and operated, and that details are added by the government as the need arises.

2. Students should be able to discuss what actions Congress and President Washington took to organize the new government.

3. Students should be able to explain how and why the Bill of Rights was added to the Constitution.

MATERIALS NEEDED

Student text

TEACHING PROCEDURES

A. Introductory Activity, Reading, and Discussion:
Reviewing student knowledge about George Washington

Introduce the lesson by asking students to relate the most important facts they know about George Washington and list this information on the chalkboard. Then have students read the "Purpose of Lesson" and "The first president" and add new facts not already listed. You might ask students why they think George Washington was often compared to Cincinnatus and sometimes portrayed by artists in Roman clothing. Washington was held by many to be a model of civic virtue and, like Cincinnatus, he retired to his home, at Mt. Vernon, after leading the victorious army of the Revolutionary War.

B. Reading and Discussion:
Understanding how Congress organized the executive branch

Have students read, "Organizing the executive branch." Students should understand the origins of the cabinet and the executive departments which were established by Congress and not provided for in the Constitution.

C. Reading and Discussion:
Understanding how Congress organized the judicial branch

Have students read "Organizing the judicial branch" and review the information provided on the court system. Have the students examine the cartoon and discuss with them the parallel state and federal judiciaries of our federal system of government. You may wish to help students understand the difference between trial courts and appellate courts.

D. Reading and Discussion:
Understanding why the Bill of Rights was drafted

Have the class read the section "The Bill of Rights." Be sure they understand the arguments of the opposing sides and the functions of the first ten amendments.

E. Concluding Activity

Have students discuss the questions under "Reviewing and using the lesson." You may wish to have them write on one of the three questions in their constitutional journals.

OPTIONAL ACTIVITIES

For Reinforcement, Extended Learning, and Enrichment

1. Have students review the first ten amendments contained in the Reference Section at the back of their text and identify their historical roots based upon what they have studied in earlier lessons and in independent research.

2. Have students bring newspaper clippings to the class that contain examples of actions taken by the executive and judicial branches of the federal government. Ask them to explain the actions and how they relate to the constitutional responsibilities of these agencies.

How did political parties develop?

LESSON OVERVIEW

In this lesson, students learn how political parties became established in the United States. Students first learn why the Framers were opposed to political parties, which they believed were "factions" concerned with selfish interests at the expense of the common welfare. Disagreements soon arose, however, between the Federalists, who were followers of Alexander Hamilton, and the Republicans, whose leader was Thomas Jefferson. These disagreements arose over the power of the national government and were focused upon how the "necessary and proper" and "general welfare" clauses of the Constitution were to be interpreted. They also involved disputes over questions of foreign policy. Political parties became established in the United States as a result of these disagreements. Students complete the lesson by learning of the functions of political parties today.

LESSON OBJECTIVES

At the conclusion of this lesson:

1. Students should be able to explain why the Framers opposed the development of political parties.

2. Students should be able to explain the basic disagreements that led to the development of the first political parties, and to identify the leadership of those parties.

3. Students should be able to describe the role and purpose of political parties.

MATERIALS NEEDED

1. Student text

2. Handout 20-1 (optional)

TEACHING PROCEDURES

A. Introductory Activity:
Speculating on the cause of political parties

Have students read the "Purpose of Lesson." Discuss the possibility of a candidate today receiving all the electoral votes. Ask students to estimate how likely this possibility is.

Ask students to speculate on what issues they think might have caused differences of opinion great enough to result in the formation of political parties. Remind students of some of the disagreements that arose during the ratification process.

B. Reading and Discussion:
Understanding disagreements that led
to the formation of political parties

Have students read the sections, "Why the Framers were against political parties" and "Disagreements between the Federalists and Republicans." Make sure students understand the basis for the Framers' resistance to political parties and the relationship of that resistance to their views on the purpose of republican government. Students could be asked to complete Handout 20-1 as a check for under-standing.

C. Problem Solving:
Understanding a dispute over the interpretation of the Constitution

To help students understand the ambiguity of the "necessary and proper" and "general welfare" clauses, have them work in small groups to answer questions included in "Problem solving." Also, discuss why the Framers included these clauses in the Constitution and the problems raised by the clauses for the principle of limited government.

D. Reading and Class Activity:
Understanding additional disputes

Before having the students read the sections on "Disagreements over the Bank of the United States," "Disagreements over foreign affairs," and "Washington's warning," you might wish to use the following problem-solving situation:

> You are a member of the governing body of a nation called Terrafirma. Two neighboring nations are at war with each other, Gaul and Albion. You must decide if Terrafirma should get involved in this war. Your nation recently gained its independence from Albion, with help from Gaul. Some of your citizens say that we should stick by our friends, the Gauls, who helped us in our time of need. Others say that since the Albionese speak our language and share our heritage, we should side with them. You have three choices: (a) side with Albion, (b) side with Gaul, (c) stay out of the war.

> Discuss with your group what recommendations to make to the governing body of Terrafirma on the Albion-Gaul war.

E. Reading and Discussion:
Understanding the functions of political parties

Have the students read the last section on "Political parties today" and review with them the ways that political parties are useful to citizens.

F. Concluding Activity

Conclude the lesson by leading a discussion of the questions included in "Reviewing and using the lesson." You might also ask students to write about what would constitute an "ideal" political party in their constitutional journals.

OPTIONAL ACTIVITIES

For Reinforcement, Extended Learning, and Enrichment

1, Have students do research to extend their timelines to show the evolution of American political parties through 1860.

2. Ask students to clip news items about political parties now active in the United States. Based on these clippings, ask students to explain the positions today's parties take on the issues that divided Hamilton and Jefferson.

3. Students may also be asked to use the clippings to create a bulletin board illustrating the various functions and positions of modern political parties.

4. Provide students with copies of the Republican and Democratic Party platforms from a recent election. Read the platforms as a group and discuss whether they confirm the Framers' view that political parties simply pursue their own interests rather than the common welfare.

Federalist or Republican?

Instructions: Put an **F** in front of each statement that describes the Federalists. Put an **R** in front of each statement that describes the Republicans.

___1.　Believed in strong local governments, as opposed to a strong national government.

___2.　Led by Thomas Jefferson.

___3.　Favored supporting the English in the war against France.

___4.　Wanted to limit the powers of Congress through a strict interpretation of the "necessary and proper" clause.

___5.　Saw an America of small independent farmers.

___6.　Believed that the "necessary and proper" clause could be broadly "read" to permit the chartering of a national bank.

___7.　Believed that the U.S. should recognize its debt to the French and support them in their war against England.

___8.　Believed that America should develop as a manufacturing and trading nation.

___9.　Led by Alexander Hamilton.

Who decides what the Constitution means?

LESSON OVERVIEW

This lesson deals with the power of the U.S. Supreme Court to exercise judicial review over the actions of state legislatures and the other two branches of the federal government. Throughout our history, there have been great differences of opinion about whether the judicial branch should have this power and how it should be used. The controversy raises basic questions about representative government on the one hand and constitutional government and the protection of basic rights and minorities on the other.

The lesson opens with a brief discussion of how students might resolve the differences of opinion about what the Constitution meant. They then read and discuss the description in the text of how the Supreme Court obtained the power of judicial review.

LESSON OBJECTIVES

At the conclusion of this lesson:

1. Students should be able to explain the right of judicial review.

2. Students should be able to describe how the Supreme Court gained the right of judicial review.

3. Students should be able to explain the differing arguments on whether the Supreme Court should have the right of judicial review.

MATERIALS NEEDED

Student text

TEACHING PROCEDURES

A. Introductory Activity:
Understanding the issues raised by the practice of judicial review

Read the "Purpose of Lesson" with the class. Help students understand the conflict regarding the power of judicial review by asking them the following questions.

1. Should the Supreme Court have the power to declare laws made by a majority vote of your representatives in Congress to be unconstitutional?

2. With what principles that you have studied would this appear to conflict?

3. What would be the advantages and disadvantages of giving the Supreme Court this power?

4. Should any other branch of government be given the power to declare unconstitutional laws passed by a majority vote of your representatives in Congress?

5. With what principles that you have studied would this appear to conflict?

6. What would be the advantages and disadvantages of not allowing anyone to overrule laws made by Congress?

B. Reading and Discussion:
Understanding how the Constitution gave the Supreme Court the power of judicial review over state governments

Although the power of judicial review is not mentioned explicitly in the Constitution, it was assumed from the time of its adoption that this power was given to the Supreme Court over actions of state governments. To help students understand this fact, have them read the sections, "Judicial review" and "Judicial review over state governments." Then discuss with students how the supremacy clause and the Judiciary Act of 1789 made clear the authority of the Court to declare actions of state governments invalid under the Constitution.

C. Reading and Discussion:
Understanding how the Supreme Court's power of judicial review was established over Congress

Have students read, "Judicial review over acts of Congress" and "*Marbury v. Madison*." Students should understand that although the Constitution does not explicitly give the Supreme Court this power, many of the Framers supported the idea. It was not until 1803 in the case of *Marbury v. Madison* that the Court claimed the power of judicial review over acts of Congress. Lead students in an examination of the case and the reasoning used by the Court to establish its power.

D. Concluding the Lesson

Conclude the lesson by leading a discussion of the questions in "Reviewing and using the lesson." Students may also be asked to record their thoughts about the power of the Supreme Court justices in their constitutional journals.

OPTIONAL ACTIVITIES

For Reinforcement, Extended Learning, and Enrichment

1. Have students read a detailed account of the *Marbury* case in a biography of Marshall or a history book. They should report the facts of the case to the class, explaining why the case was so politically sensitive.

2. Review with the students the origins of the two political parties and the positions of Hamilton and Jefferson on the interpretation of the Constitution. Give the following quotations to the class and ask them to identify the author or the political party:

    "... the opinion which gives to the judges the right to decide what laws are constitutional, and what not ... would make the Judiciary a despotic branch." (Thomas Jefferson)

    "... the judiciary, from the nature of its functions, will always be the least dangerous. ... It may truly be said to have neither Force nor Will, but merely judgement. ... A constitution is, in fact, and must be regarded by the judges, as a fundamental law. It therefore belongs to them to ascertain its meaning ..." (Alexander Hamilton)

How does the Supreme Court interpret the Constitution?

LESSON OVERVIEW

This brief lesson presents students with differing approaches used to interpret the meaning of the Constitution. Students are asked to identify the advantages and disadvantages of each means described.

LESSON OBJECTIVES

At the conclusion of this lesson:

1. Students should be able to explain three commonly used approaches to deciding the meaning of the Constitution.

2. Students should be able to describe the advantages and disadvantages associated with the three approaches to deciding the meaning of the Constitution.

MATERIALS NEEDED

Student text

TEACHING PROCEDURES

A. Introductory Activity:
Reviewing the Hamilton /Jefferson controversy over interpreting the Constitution

Review with students the controversy between Jefferson and Hamilton over the interpretation of the necessary and proper clause of the Constitution. You might wish to ask students to identify what problems might be involved in interpreting the meaning of such clauses from the Constitution as "due process of law," "unreasonable searches and seizures," or the prohibition against "cruel or unusual punishment." Conclude by asking students what means they think should be used to interpret the meaning of the Constitution and list the means they suggest on the chalkboard.

B. Reading and Group Activity:
Understanding different methods of interpretation

Have students read the entire lesson. Then, divide the class into groups of three to five students each and assign each group the task of identifying the advantages and disadvantages of one of the three means of interpreting the Constitution described in the text. Students may be encouraged to support their positions with excerpts from the Constitution contained in the Reference Section. When the groups are prepared, have them present their positions to the rest of the class for discussion.

C. Concluding Activity.

Have students answer the questions in "Reviewing and using the lesson." You may wish to have them write about one of the three main approaches in their constitutional journals.

OPTIONAL ACTIVITIES

For Reinforcement, Extended Learning, and Enrichment

1. Have students bring clippings from news media to class that illustrate conflicts over the proper means of interpreting the Constitution.

2. Have students research the arguments about constitutional interpretation that were made in confirmation hearings of nominees to the Supreme Court and report their findings to the class.

Unit Five

How does the Constitution protect our basic rights?

UNIT OVERVIEW

This unit focuses on five basic rights protected by the Constitution—freedom of expression, freedom of religion, the right to vote, equal protection, and due process. The lessons focus not only on the importance of these rights but on how they have been expanded over the past two hundred years. Students begin by examining the rights to freedom of expression and freedom of religion, the reasons the Founders thought their protection was especially important, and the ways in which this protection has been applied in various instances.

The text reviews the history of the right to vote. Particular emphasis is given to the expansion of the franchise to groups that previously were denied this right. Students learn that this extension has been accomplished by constitutional amendments, judicial decisions, and legislative enactments at both the state and federal levels.

The last two lessons in the unit look at the equal protection and due process clauses. Students learn how the equal protection clause of the Fourteenth Amendment has been used to eliminate legalized discrimination against minorities. Students then learn how the due process clauses of the Fifth and Fourteenth Amendments have been used to protect individual liberty from unfair encroachment by the federal and state governments.

UNIT OBJECTIVES

At the conclusion of this unit:

1. Students should be able to describe the different forms of freedom of expression and their importance, both to the individual and to the preservation of constitutional democracy. They should also be able to explain why it is necessary sometimes to impose limits on freedom of expression.

2. Students should be able to explain the importance to the Founders of freedom of religion, describe situations in which religious practices may be limited, and explain the present position of the Supreme Court on the relationship between religion and the schools.

3. Students should be able to describe how the right to vote has been expanded and why this is important.

4. Students should be able to describe what equal protection of the law means, and how it has been used to eliminate legalized discrimination against various minorities.

5. Students should be able to describe what due process is, why it is important in a constitutional democracy, and how the concept has been applied to the rights of juveniles who are accused of breaking the law.

How does the Constitution protect freedom of expression?

LESSON OVERVIEW

In this lesson students learn about the relationship of freedom of expression to political freedom. Students first read and discuss the freedom of expression portion of the First Amendment. Students learn that this section of the amendment is designed to protect various forms of freedom of expression. They then read and discuss why freedom of expression was viewed as so important by the Founders and explore some of the principal arguments in support of this freedom. Finally, students learn that there are limits on this important freedom when it conflicts with other important rights and interests. The relevance of this right to their own experiences is demonstrated by a reading and discussion of two Supreme Court cases dealing with students' rights to freedom of expression.

LESSON OBJECTIVES

At the conclusion of this lesson:

1. Students should be able to describe the freedoms included under the First Amendment's guarantee of freedom of expression.

2. Students should be able to describe some of the historical incidents that influenced the Founders' position on freedom of expression.

3. Students should be able to explain the benefits of freedom of expression.

4. Students should be able to give reasons for placing limits on freedom of expression.

5. Students should be able to formulate and defend an opinion on whether freedom of expression should be limited in a particular case.

MATERIALS NEEDED

1. Student text

2. Handout 23-1 (optional)

TEACHING PROCEDURES

A. Introductory Activity:
Introducing the First Amendment

Have students read the "Purpose of Lesson" and "What is freedom of expression?" Then review with students the excerpts from the First Amendment included in their text, being sure they understand what each clause relating to freedom of expression means. Remind students that they can look in the glossary for the meaning of terms they are unfamiliar with.

Discuss the following questions.

- What basic rights are listed in this portion of the First Amendment?
- Why do you think these particular rights were included?
- Why do you think they were included in this first amendment to the Constitution and not in a later one?

B. Reading and Discussion:
Understanding the importance of freedom of expression

Have the class read the sections, "Why was freedom of expression so important to the Founders?" and "What are some of the benefits of freedom of expression?" In discussing the text, be sure students understand the relationship of freedom of expression to political freedom and the arguments commonly given for the importance of this right.

C. Reading and Discussion:
Deciding when freedom of discussion should be limited

Read with the class the section, "When should freedom of expression be limited?" Ask students to think of situations in which they think freedom of expression might endanger other important values and interests such as national security or public safety. Then discuss with the students other rights that we value that might conflict with freedom of expression, such as the right to privacy and the right to a fair trial.

D. Reading and Group Activity:
Dealing with issues of freedom of expression

Read the section on "Freedom of expression in the schools" with the students. This section summarizes the facts and rulings in the well-known *Tinker* case [*Tinker v. Des Moines School District*, 393 U.S. 503 (1969)]. Then have students complete the "Problem Solving" activity that follows which discusses the 1988 Supreme Court case *Hazelwood School District v. Kuhlmeier*, (88 Daily Journal D.A.R. 564). Divide the class into groups of three to five students each. Ask each group to read both of the cases presented in the text and (1) identify the competing rights and interests they involve, and (2) explain which rights and interests the group thinks should be given priority in each situation.

Then explain to the class that the Court ruled in favor of the principal in the *Hazelwood* case. In the *Hazelwood* case, in a five to three decision, the Court overturned a lower court decision and upheld the school district's right to censor the school newspaper. The newspaper was written and edited by a journalism class, as part of the school's curriculum. Therefore, the Court said, it was not to be considered as a forum for public expression and school officials may impose reasonable restrictions, such as protecting the privacy of pregnant students. Dissenting justices said that the articles deleted by the principal would not have disrupted classroom work nor invaded the rights of others, and were therefore covered by First Amendment protections of freedom of expression.

E. Concluding Activity

Conclude the lesson by leading a discussion of the questions contained in "Reviewing and using the lesson." You also may wish to have the students select one of the freedoms of expression protected by the First Amendment and write a paragraph in their constitutional journals explaining why this freedom is still important today.

OPTIONAL ACTIVITIES

For Reinforcement, Extended Learning, and Enrichment

1. Have the students read the expanded case study, *Tinker v. Des Moines Independent School District* (1969), on Handout 23-1 (immediately following) and discuss its relevance to them and the Constitution. Focus the discussion on some of the reasons why freedom of expression is important and the difference that it might make for their lives.

2. Have students look in magazines and newspapers for articles about contemporary issues of freedom of expression. Have them analyze the articles and create a bulletin board that illustrates a First Amendment theme in today's news.

3. Invite representatives from a newspaper, television station, or radio station to class to talk about the limits government has placed on their freedom of expression. What public interests are these limits designed to protect? Do they feel the limits are justified? Why or why not?

4. If your school has a student-run newspaper, you might ask members of the staff, the faculty adviser, and the school principal to conduct a panel discussion for your class, focusing not only on the recent Supreme Court decision but also on any disagreements or censorship incidents that have occurred in your school. What educational goals have conflicted or might conflict with freedom of expression?

5. Interested students might research cases after the Tinker case dealing with symbolic speech — wearing of headgear or insignia, the use of the American flag on clothing, etc., or the right to free assembly (creating and operating student clubs on campus).

6. Tell students that they are about to take part in an activity that will demonstrate what life might be like in a country without First Amendment rights. Choose one of the following activities to use with the class or divide the class into groups and assign each group one of the activities.

Activity A — "Control the press"

a. Appoint a "Censorship Board" of three class members. They are controlled by only one rule: **Any information allowed to leave the classroom must make the teacher and her/his decisions look good.** Failure to follow this rule will result in a call home and a trip to the principal's office. (Suggest that the new rules are in response to a new schoolwide policy aimed at helping students do better in school.)

b. Appoint four "members of the Free World Press" and have them wait in another classroom for a few minutes.

c. Announce to the class the following three new rules:

   - Anyone talking without permission will get 30 minutes detention.
   - Anyone arguing with the teacher will get 30 minutes detention.
   - Anyone leaving his or her seat for any reason during the class period will get 30 minutes detention.

   Explain that these new rules are designed to keep better order in the classroom. Have pairs of students, acting as reporters, write headlines and brief articles summarizing for the "outside world" (rest of the school or school newspaper) the new rules governing their classroom.

d.   Announce that the Censorship Board will impose punishments for negative articles. If the Censorship Board is unwilling to establish meaningful punishments, they will have to accept the consequences mentioned above. The Censorship Board should then choose the article that shows the teacher and the new rules in the best light as the official version of events. It should also impose penalties on those groups that reported unfavorably on the teacher or the new rules.

e.   Members of the "Free World Press" should then reenter the room and be given the officially accepted version of events. They should write a brief account of the three new rules as they have been allowed to see them.

f.   Discuss the situation by asking the following questions:

   • How would you compare the censored version of events with the actual events?
   • What did you think of the new rules?
   • What would you want to include in an article you were writing about the event?
   • Did the fear of punishment keep you from saying what you wanted to in your article?
   • How do you think fear of punishment affects the press in countries that do not have a free press?
   • Do you think that a Censorship Board is even needed, or would fear keep people from printing what they want?

Activity B — "Divide and conquer"

a.   Put up a poster with the following three "new rules."

   • Anyone talking without permission will get 30 minutes detention.
   • Anyone arguing with the teacher will get 30 minutes detention.
   • Anyone leaving his or her seat for any reason during the class period will get 30 minutes detention.

b.   Allow students to create informal gatherings to discuss the fairness of the new rules.

c.   Tell them that if they can develop a classwide alternative to the rules given, they might be able to convince the teacher to change the rules.

d.   Immediately change your mind about allowing the "assemblies" to take place, citing a need for better order, which was the reason for the rules in the first place.

e.   Solicit individual, written suggestions for change. Suggest that there will be serious steps taken to deal with anyone who suggests something too radical or with critical overtones.

f.   Discuss the fears and frustrations of working alone to confront repressive authority as compared to working with a group.

g.   Discuss the activity using the following questions:

   • How did you feel when you were told you couldn't work together?
   • Did the fear of punishment keep you from arguing about the restriction on group activity?
   • What were the benefits and costs of working alone?
   • What would be the benefits and costs of working with a group?

Activity C—"Suppressing discussion and thought"

a. Announce the three new class rules noted above. Do not allow discussion.

b. Assign a short group assignment of your choosing. Reading the student text for this lesson would be appropriate.

c. Tell the students that they may discuss the assignment but they are not to discuss the new rules. ("It's just something that was necessary for a more orderly and efficient classroom!") Also warn them that there are students throughout the room who have been asked to report instances of unauthorized discussion to you, in secret, at a later time. There will be an un-named consequence, depending on the severity of the offense, for those who are reported.

d. After providing a few minutes to complete the group work, move on to a discussion.

e. Discuss the activity using the following questions:

- Was it hard to refrain from discussing the new rules?
- Did you discuss them anyway? If not, why not? If you did, were you worried about being reported?
- Are there countries where adults face the same problems in discussing and criticizing their government that you just faced with the new rules? Can you name some?
- How can people express their opinions in those countries and avoid being punished by the government? Were there really any "spies" in our class? Does this tell us that sometimes the fear of being caught acts to keep people from speaking freely?

HANDOUT 23-1

Tinker v. Des Moines Independent School District (1969)

In December, 1965, a small group of students and their parents decided to express their opposition to the United States' involvement in the Vietnam War by wearing black armbands for about two weeks during the holiday season. Some of the group had participated in similar protest activities before, including Mr. Tinker, a Methodist minister; Mrs. Eckhardt, an official in the Women's International League for Peace and Freedom; and the children of both families. They said the protest would include wearing the armbands to school.

The principals of the Des Moines public schools heard of the plan, and on December 15 adopted a policy specifically prohibiting students from wearing black armbands while at school, and announced the policy in the schools. The Tinker and Eckhardt children knew of the schools' policy. They understood they would be suspended if they disobeyed the rule. On December 16 and 17, seven of the 18,000 students enrolled in the Des Moines public school system wore the black armbands. They attended classes as usual. There were no overt disruptions of classroom activities, no demonstrations, and no threats of violence. Outside the classroom, however, a few angry remarks were directed toward the students with armbands. And a mathematics teacher reported that his lesson period had been practically "wrecked by disputes" with Mary Beth Tinker.

Later in the afternoon, the students wearing the armbands were called into the principal's office and asked to remove them. When they refused, they were suspended until they returned to school without the armbands. John F. Tinker, age 15, and Mary Beth Tinker, age 13, were among the five students suspended. After the planned protest period was over, the students returned to school.

After the suspension, school authorities had prepared a statement listing the reasons for banning black armbands. The statement referred to the fact that a former student, whose friends were still in school, had been killed in Vietnam and that "if any kind of demonstration existed, it might evolve into something which would be hard to control." The school authorities said that the regulation was directed "against the principle of demonstration" itself, that "schools are no places for demonstrations," and "if students didn't like the way our elected officials were handling things, it should be handled with the ballot box and not in the halls of our public schools." They also said their decision to ban black armbands—symbols of opposition to American involvement in Vietnam—was influenced by the fact that the Vietnam War had recently become "the subject of major controversy"—as indicated by mass marches in Washington and draft card burning incidents.

Mr. Tinker filed a complaint on behalf of his children that their right of free expression had been violated. He asked for a small amount of money and requested that the children not be disciplined for their actions.

The case finally reached the Supreme Court, and the Court ruled in the students' favor. Mr. Justice Fortas, writing the majority opinion of the Court, said:

> First Amendment rights...are available to teachers and students. It can hardly be argued that either students or teachers shed their constitutional rights to freedom of speech or expression at the schoolhouse gate....Under our Constitution, free speech is not a right that is given only to be so circumscribed that it exists in principle but not in fact....The Constitution says that Congress (and the States) may not abridge the right to free speech. This provision means what it says.

Reviewing and using the case

1. What does this selection have to do with the Constitution?

2. How does this case show the relevance of the Constitution to your life?

3. Under what circumstances do you think it would be reasonable and fair to limit students' rights to express their political opinions in school?

How does the Constitution protect freedom of religion?

LESSON OVERVIEW

Many of the colonies gave preferential treatment to certain churches. By the time of the Constitution's ratification, however, many in the new nation believed that the federal government should not be allowed to give such status to any one church. Furthermore, many thought that people have a "natural right" to believe whatever they choose. Thus, a part of the First Amendment says that "Congress shall make no law respecting the establishment of religion, or prohibiting the free exercise thereof, . . ."

Students first learn why the Founders thought freedom of religion was so important. Then they learn of the conflicts over the interpretation and application of the "establishment" and "free exercise" clauses of the First Amendment. Students learn that the Supreme Court has ruled that while people have the right to hold any belief or no belief, their religious practices can be limited when those practices interfere with other public interests. And, finally, they read a selection about limits on freedom of religion and apply the "Lemon test" — a set of criteria the Supreme Court has developed for use in determining whether laws involving religion are constitutional — to several situations.

LESSON OBJECTIVES

At the conclusion of this lesson:

1. Students should be able to explain why the Founders thought freedom of religion was important.

2. Students should be able to explain the differences between the establishment and the free exercise clauses of the First Amendment.

3. Students should be able to describe reasons for limits on religious practices.

4. Students should be able to apply the Lemon test to cases involving religion and the public schools.

MATERIALS NEEDED

Student text

TEACHING PROCEDURES

A. Reading and Discussion:
Understanding the Founders' beliefs about freedom of religion

Have students read the "Purpose of Lesson" and "Why did the Founders think freedom of religion was important?" Help them understand the factors that contributed to the growth of religious tolerance among the Founders. This should include an understanding of the influence of the ideas they derived from the natural rights philosophy on their idea of the proper role of government in regard to religious beliefs and practices. It should also include an understanding of the Founders' beliefs about the role of religion in the development of the character traits required of republican government.

B. Reading and Discussion:
Understanding the bases of conflicts regarding freedom of religion
and the proper role of government

Have students read and discuss the next two sections, "Conflicts over freedom of religion" and "Conflicts between the establishment and the free exercise clauses." Help students understand the differences between the establishment and free exercise clauses and the conflicts over their interpretation and application. Have the students identify the public interests with which several of the religious practices mentioned in the text would conflict.

C. Reading and Problem Solving:
Dealing with problems of freedom of religion

Have the students read "Should the government be allowed to support religious education?" Discuss the three questions posed.

For each criterion in the Lemon test, ask one student to paraphrase it and another to create an imaginary law that would violate it.

Then, divide the class into groups of three to five. Have each group read the situations in the "Problem Solving" exercise and apply the Lemon test to decide whether the laws and actions cited should be declared unconstitutional. If it can be reproduced for the class, the students can use the reference handout at the end of this lesson for research to support their decisions. Have the groups report their decisions and explain the reasoning they applied to reach their decision in each situation.

D. Concluding Activity

Conclude the lesson by leading a discussion of the questions provided in "Reviewing and using the lesson." You may wish to have students write their positions on one of the constitutional issues dealing with the freedom of religion in their constitutional journals.

OPTIONAL ACTIVITIES

For Reinforcement, Extended Learning, and Enrichment

1. Have students discuss the position that if, as George Washington and other Founders thought, free government depends on virtue and morality, and if they cannot be maintained without religion, our federal and state governments should promote and encourage religion in general, though no one religion in particular.

2. Have students discuss and take positions on the following quotations.

    > Believing with you that religion is a matter which lies solely between man and his God, that he owes account to none other for his faith or his worship... I contemplate with sovereign reverence that act of the whole American people which declared that their legislature should "make no law respecting an establishment of religion, or prohibiting the free exercise thereof," thus building a wall of separation between Church and State... (Thomas Jefferson, Letter to the Danbury Baptist Association, 1802).

    > We are a religious people whose institutions presuppose a Supreme Being....When the state encourages religious instruction...it follows the best of our traditions. For it then respects the religious nature of our people and accommodates the public service to their spiritual needs. (Justice William O. Douglas, *Zorach v. Clauson*, 1952).

3. Have a student report on the religious ideas of Roger Williams, Ann Hutchinson, or Thomas Hooker.

4. Ask several students to find out and report to the class what positions local religious organizations take on the question of prayer in the public schools and the need for a constitutional amendment on this issue.

Reference Section for Problem Solving Situations

1. In *Stone v. Graham* 101 S.Ct. 192(1980), the Supreme Court ruled in a 5-4 decision that a Kentucky law allowing the display of the Ten Commandments in classrooms was unconstitutional.

2. In *Mueller v. Allen* 103 S.Ct. 3062(1983), the Supreme Court in a 5-4 decision allowed Minnesota tax deductions to parents of both public and private/parochial students for educational expenses.

3. In *Aguilar v. Felton* 105 S.Ct. 3248(1985), the Supreme Court voided in a 5-4 decision two programs in New York and Michigan that sent public school teachers to parochial schools to provide remedial instruction.

4. In *Widmer v. Vincent* 102 S.Ct. 269(1981), the Supreme Court by a 8-1 vote held that college officials may not deny student religious groups access to campus facilities. However, the Court has failed to decide a case involving high school students [*Brandon v. Board of Education* 635 F.2d 971(1980) and *Bender v. Williamsport Area School District* 106 S.Ct. 1326(1986)].

Additional Background on the Cases

No. 1: Ten Commandments Case
Citation: *Stone v. Graham,* 101 S.Ct. 192 (1980) 66 L.Ed.2d. 199

Issue: Does the posting of a copy of the Ten Commandments in public school classrooms violate the establishment clause of the Constitution?

Facts: The state of Kentucky passed a law requiring all classrooms to post a copy of the Ten Commandments. The state argued that "secular application of the Ten Commandments is clearly seen in its adoption as the fundamental legal code of Western Civilization and the Common Law of the United States." The copies would be financed through voluntary contributions.

The state law was sustained by a state trial court and was affirmed by a tie vote of the state supreme court.

Decision: In a 5-4 opinion, the state law was overturned with Justices Brennan, White, Marshall, Powell, and Stevens constituting the majority. The Court said, "The Ten Commandmants are undeniably a sacred text in the Jewish and Christian faiths, and no legislative recitation of a supposedly secular purpose can blind us to that fact."

No. 2: Tax Deductions
Citation: *Mueller v. Allen,* 103 S.Ct. 3062 (1983) 77 L.Ed.2d. 721

Issue: Is the establishment clause of the First Amendment violated if a state provides state income tax deductions for educational expenses to parochial schools?

Facts: The Minnesota state legislature passed a law, granting a tax deduction to parents for school expenses in the areas of tuition, transportation, and educational materials at public and private/parochial schools. A cap of $500 for K-6 expenses and $700 for 7-12 expenses was written into the law. 91,000 of

820,000 students in Minnesota were enrolled in private schools, and 95% of that 91,000 were attending parochial schools.

Decision: In a 5-4 decision, Justice Rehnquist for the majority, argued that there was no violation of the *Lemon* test. He noted that Minnesota law provided a wide variety of tax deductions and that this particular deduction was not giving special treatment to parochial school parents but was open to all parents of school- age children. He also argued that the effect of the tax deductions was a well-educated citizenry, which was constitutionally permitted.

No. 3: Public School Teachers in Parochial Schools
Citation: *Aguilar v. Felton,* 105 S.Ct. 3248 (1985) 87 L.Ed.2d. 290

Issue: Can public schools provide instruction in a parochial school setting?

Facts: New York City schools had regularly used Title I funds to send their teachers into parochial schools to provide remedial math, reading, and English instruction during the school day. Grand Rapids schools provided a similar program that offered a wider range of subjects and included paying rent to the parochial schools for the use of their classrooms during the instructional period.

The concept of "shared time" was used in the arguments before the Court. These students were said to be enrolled part-time in the public school and part-time in the parochial school. In both cases, these parochial school classrooms were designated as being public school classrooms and all religious symbols had been draped or removed.

Decision: In a 5-4 decision, Justice Brennan found that the program would cause "excessive entanglement" of the church and state, since teachers would have to be supervised to make sure that no religious instruction was being provided.

No. 4: Equal Access to School Facilities
Citations: *Widmer v. Vincent,* 102 S.Ct. 269 (1981)
Brandon v. Board of Education, 635 F.2d 971 (1980)
Bender v. Williamsport Area School District, 106 S.Ct.1326 (1986)
Lubbock Independent School Board v. Lubbock ACLU, 669 F.2d. 1038 (1982)

Issue: Can schools allow student religious groups the use of school facilities on the same basis as any other student groups on campus?

Facts: In the *Widmer* case, a student religious group at the University of Kansas City had been able to use the campus facilities from 1973-77, although the university had a 1972 regulation that banned the use of campus facilities for the purpose of religious worship or religious teaching. Starting in 1978, the school officials decided to enforce this rule, and rejected the group's future use of campus facilities. The college students filed a suit, claiming violation of their constitutional rights under the First Amendment.

In the *Brandon* case, several students asked the principal for permission to conduct voluntary prayers prior to the start of school each day. The principal, the superintendent, and the school board rejected the request. The students filed a suit, claiming that their rights to free exercise of religion, free speech, and free assembly were being violated.

In the *Bender* case, a student religious group asked to meet during the school's activity period to discuss religion as well as to conduct voluntary prayers. School officials rejected their request and the students filed a suit, claiming that their constitutional rights to freely exercise their religion, to free speech, and to freely assemble had been violated.

In the *Lubbock* case, the school board had allowed school prayers and Bible readings over school public address systems. In addition, Bibles had been distributed to elementary students. The school board was ordered by a U.S. Court of Appeals to stop these practices. As a result, the school board adopted a policy that allowed student groups (including religious ones) to use school facilities for meetings as long as attendance at such meetings was voluntary.

Decisions: In the *Widmer* case, the Supreme Court ruled 8-1 that the college students' rights were being violated because religious and nonreligious speech are protected. (1981)

In the *Brandon* case, the District Court dismissed the case and the Court of Appeals affirmed that dismissal. The appellate court noted that public schools do not have the tradition of being public forums that colleges and universities have, and that students still could freely exercise their religion, although not in a school setting. The U.S. Supreme Court refused to hear the case. (1980)

In the *Bender* case, the students won in District Court but lost in the Court of Appeals. The U.S. Supreme Court ruled that Bender had no standing since he was no longer on the school board nor a parent of one of the affected students. The case was sent back to the U.S. District Court. (1986)

In the *Lubbock* case, the Court of Appeals found that the new policy was a violation of the establishment clause and stated that no use of public school facilities for meetings of student religious groups before or after school hours was constitutionally permissible. The U.S. Supreme Court refused to hear the case. (1983)

How has the right to vote expanded since the Constitution was adopted?

LESSON OVERVIEW

This lesson focuses upon the right to vote and how it has expanded since the colonial period. The expansion has been so great, in fact, that further extension is no longer a serious political issue. Rather, the focus is upon upgrading the quality and quantity of participation of those who already have the right to vote.

Students learn of the early restrictions of the right to vote and of its gradual extension to those previously denied the right.

LESSON OBJECTIVES

At the conclusion of this lesson:

1. Students should be able to list groups who were denied suffrage in the past.

2. Students should be able to explain how voting restrictions for various groups in the United States were lifted.

3. Students should be able to explain why the federal government became involved in regulating voting.

MATERIALS NEEDED

1. Student text

2. Handouts 25-1 and 25-2

TEACHING PROCEDURES

A. Introductory Activity:
Understanding principles underlying the right to vote

Begin discussion by asking students:

Suppose all members of the class had collected money from their parents for a class party. Then the teacher ruled that only those students whose parents had contributed $5.00 or more could take part in deciding how the money should be spent.

- What, if anything, is unfair about this situation?
- What ideas that you have studied would this violate?

B. Reading, Discussion, and Problem Solving:
Understanding early restrictions on voting

Have students read the "Purpose of Lesson" and the section "Extending the right to vote to all white males." Ask why students think requirements such as owning property or belonging to a certain religion were placed on voting rights in this early period. Were these restrictions consistent with the ideals of our form of government?

Then, have students work individually or in pairs to read the "Problem Solving" exercise. Depending on the time available, you may have them write their editorials in class or decide on a position during class and do the writing as a homework assignment.

C. Reading, Problem Solving, and Discussion:
Understanding early state restrictions

Have students read "Extending the right to vote to black males." Allow time for students to complete the "Problem Solving" exercise individually. Describe to the class what each of the exclusionary devices was and how it was used to deny black citizens the right to vote. Discuss why it was necessary for the national government to take steps in enfranchising blacks.

D. Reading and Discussion:
Understanding the federal role in extending voting rights

Have students read the remainder of the text. Focus discussion on the role of the federal government in relation to the extension of voting rights.

E. Concluding Activity

Conclude the lesson by leading a discussion of the ideas embodied in the illustrations in this lesson of the student text. Then, discuss the questions provided in "Reviewing and using the lesson." You may wish to have students write responses to selected questions in their constitutional journals. One such question could be "What restrictions, if any, do you think the states should impose on voting rights?"

OPTIONAL ACTIVITIES

For Reinforcement, Extended Learning, and Enrichment

1. Distribute Handout 25-1 to students and have them complete the maps and answer the accompanying questions. The data provided on the information sheet can be placed on a computer data base or given to the students as a reference sheet. If you wish to have students answer the research questions at the end of the handout, you will need to make sources available to them.

2. Distribute Handout 25-2 and have students assess the generalizations based on the maps they completed in Handout 25-1. Generalizations 1, 3, 4, 5, 7, 8, 11, 12, 13, 15, 16, and 18 should be marked with a plus sign; generalizations 2, 9, 10, and 17 should be marked with a minus sign. Generalizations 6 and 14 are accurate, but the data provided is not sufficient to reach this conclusion.

3. Have students find out about your state's restrictions on the right to vote. They might also survey adults to find out how many are registered to vote and did, in fact, vote in the last election. Students could then discuss reasons for low registration and/or turnout. Does this indicate that the right to vote is taken for granted? That people do not care about the government? That people are satisfied with the way the government is running and therefore feel voting is unnecessary? That people think their vote is not important?

The Growth of Democracy

Instructions:

Part I: Use the information sheet to color code the three maps. Each map represents a different census year, i.e., 1820, 1830, and 1840.

1820

1830

1840

Map Key:

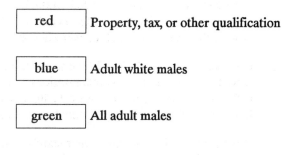

red	Property, tax, or other qualification
blue	Adult white males
green	All adult males

Information Sheet
Voting Qualifications by State

1820-1840

STATE	1820	1830	1840
Alabama	Adult white males	Adult white males	Adult white males
Arkansas			Adult white males
Connecticut	Property, tax, or other	Property, tax, or other	Property, tax, or other
Delaware	Property, tax, or other	Property, tax, or other	Property, tax, or other
Georgia	Property, tax, or other	Property, tax, or other	Property, tax, or other
Illinois	Adult white males	Adult white males	Adult white males
Indiana	Adult white males	Adult white males	Adult white males
Kentucky	Adult white males	Adult white males	Adult white males
Louisiana	Property, tax, or other	Adult white males	Adult white males
Maine	Property, tax, or other	All adult males	All adult males
Maryland	Adult white males	Adult white males	Adult white males
Massachusetts	Property, tax, or other	Property, tax, or other	Property, tax, or other
Michigan			Adult white males
Mississippi	Property, tax, or other	Property, tax, or other	Adult white males
Missouri		Adult white males	Adult white males
New Hampshire	Property, tax, or other	Property, tax, or other	Property, tax, or other
New Jersey	Property, tax, or other	Property, tax, or other	Property, tax, or other
New York	Property, tax, or other	Adult white males	Adult white males
North Carolina	Property, tax, or other	Property, tax, or other	Property, tax, or other
Ohio	Property, tax, or other	Property, tax, or other	Property, tax, or other
Pennsylvania	Property, tax, or other	Property, tax, or other	Property, tax, or other
Rhode Island	Property, tax, or other	Property, tax, or other	Property, tax, or other
South Carolina	Property, tax, or other	Property, tax, or other	Property, tax, or other
Tennessee	Property, tax, or other	Property, tax, or other	Adult white males
Vermont	All adult males	All adult males	All adult males
Virginia	Property, tax, or other	Property, tax, or other	Property, tax, or other

Part II. Answer the following questions based on the maps you have completed.

1. How many states had property, tax, or other voting qualifications in 1820? _____
    In 1830? _____ In 1840?_____

2. How many states allowed all adult white males to vote in 1820? _____ In 1830? _____
    In 1840? _____

3. How many states allowed all adult males to vote in 1820? _____ In 1830? _____ In 1840? _____

4. Which part of the country had the fewest voting restrictions?_____

5. How many new states were added to the United States between 1820 and 1840? _____ What
    were the voting qualifications in these new states?

6. After completing the maps on the growth of democracy, what did you learn about voting rights
    between 1820 and 1840?

    _____

    _____

    _____

Part III. Research the answers to these questions.

7. Between 1820 and 1840, how were average people able to be involved in government?

    _____

    _____

    _____

8. Find evidence to support the following statement: "More than any other person, Jackson stood
    for the growing power of the people in government."

    _____

    _____

    _____

The Growth of Democracy

Generalizations

Use the maps you colored to evaluate the following generalizations. Put a plus sign (+) in the blank for generalizations that are accurate. Put a minus sign (-) by those statements which are **contradicted** by the maps. Put a question mark (?) in the blank if there is not enough information on the maps to make a judgment.

_____ 1. In 1820, most states required a person to own property, pay taxes, or meet some similar qualification in order to vote.

_____ 2. More states had property qualifications for voting in 1840 than in 1830.

_____ 3. In 1830, the states that had the fewest restrictions on voting were in the Northeast.

_____ 4. By 1840, the West was more democratic than the East.

_____ 5. In 1830, the North was more democratic than the South.

_____ 6. Women were not allowed to vote in any state in 1840.

_____ 7. The new states admitted to the U.S. between 1820 and 1840 had fewer voting restrictions than the older states.

_____ 8. In 1820, Tennessee required a person to own property in order to vote.

_____ 9. Pennsylvania changed its voting requirements between 1820 and 1840.

_____ 10. Alabama allowed all adult males to vote in all three census years.

_____ 11. Maine changed its voting requirements between 1820 and 1830.

_____ 12. In 1840, Mississippi allowed all adult white males to vote.

_____ 13. Most of the original 13 states still had property requirements for voting in 1840.

_____ 14. Michigan was admitted to the U.S. between 1830 and 1840.

_____ 15. Only white men were allowed to vote in most states in 1840.

_____ 16. Black males were allowed to vote in only two states in 1830.

_____ 17. Some states increased the restrictions on voting between 1820 and 1840.

_____ 18. More people were eligible to vote in the Western states than in the Eastern states in 1840.

What is the right to equal protection of the laws?

LESSON OVERVIEW

The Fourteenth Amendment was enacted to prevent discrimination against blacks after the Civil War. Because of the way in which the amendment was interpreted by legislators and the courts, however, discrimination persisted for many years following its enactment. In the late 1800s, the Supreme Court in the case of *Plessy v. Ferguson* legitimized the doctrine that "separate but equal" facilities did not constitute unconstitutional discrimination. It was not until 1954, in the *Brown v. Board of Education* case, that the Court overruled this decision, stating that separate educational facilities are inherently unequal. Since that time, efforts by blacks and other groups have brought about legislative changes that have extended equal protection of the laws to groups that have traditionally been discriminated against.

The lesson opens with a problem-solving discussion of five examples of discrimination. Students then read and discuss the text, which traces the development of equal protection from 1868 to the present.

LESSON OBJECTIVES

At the conclusion of this lesson:

1. Students should be able to explain the purpose of the Fourteenth Amendment, particularly the equal protection clause.

2. Students should be able to compare the findings in *Plessy v. Ferguson* and *Brown v. Board of Education* and explain the importance of the change in the Supreme Court's position.

3. Students should be able to explain important events in the national movement to end discrimination.

MATERIALS NEEDED

1. Student text

2. Handout 26-1 (optional)

TEACHING PROCEDURES

A. Introductory Problem Solving: Identifying examples of unfair discrimination

Inform students that the equal protection clause of the Fourteenth Amendment requires that all people be treated equally under federal and state laws. Then have students read and discuss the "Purpose of Lesson" and five examples of discrimination in the "Problem Solving" exercise. Ask students to take and defend positions on whether they think the types of situations contained in the exercise should be considered unconstitutional under the equal protection clause. You might ask students if they know whether any of these practices have actually been declared unconstitutional by the Supreme Court. Conclude by asking students to explain what they think might be the importance of the equal protection clause for themselves.

B. Reading and Discussion:
Understanding the changing interpretations of "equal protection"

Have students read "The Fourteenth Amendment and equal protection of the laws" and "The Supreme Court and equal protection." Lead students in a discussion of the two court cases and the changed social, economic, and political conditions that may have influenced the Court's decision in the *Brown* case. Ask students to give their opinions as to whether the *Brown* case ended discrimination.

C. Reading and Discussion:
Understanding continuing problems of equal protection

Have students read "Ending discrimination." Discuss the role of the federal government in the *Brown* case and the importance of citizen participation in reducing unfair discrimination. You may wish to conclude this section by discussing with students the limits of the law in reducing prejudice and unfair discrimination, and the advantages and disadvantages of this task being undertaken by other means. For example, you may wish to discuss the importance in this effort of the schools, the church, and other community groups.

D. Concluding Activity

Conclude the lesson by leading a class discussion of the questions contained in "Reviewing and using the lesson."

OPTIONAL ACTIVITIES

For Reinforcement, Extended Learning, and Enrichment

1. If you have posters or photographs depicting slogans or particular forms of protest used in the civil rights movement, display these for students. Have students compile a list of the slogans and forms of protest used to fight prejudice, those used to combat discrimination, and those aimed at both. Students might then be asked to identify the advantages and disadvantages of the different forms of participation.

2. Point out that the *Brown v. Board of Education* decision was unanimous, while the *Plessy v. Ferguson* decision was not. Why might it be important for a controversial decision, especially one that overturned a previous Court decision, to be unanimous?

3. Encourage interested class members to read some of the recollections of the first black students to attend previously all-white schools. What was the experience like? Did the students face discrimination?

Ending Discrimination

1. Below are some important events in our nation's struggle to end discrimination. The dates for some events are missing. Find these dates in your text and add them to your list.

2. Put the events listed on the timeline on the next page.

3. Study your timeline carefully. Does it provide any insight into the right to equal protection?

List of Events

Thirteenth Amendment ratified (   )

Fourteenth Amendment ratified (   )

Fifteenth Amendment ratified (   )

Ex-Confederates regained control of state legislatures in the Southern states (1869-1877)

Southern states passed segregation laws (1880-1895)

Supreme Court upheld "separate but equal" facilities (   )

President Roosevelt issued an executive order banning discrimination in hiring by defense contractors (1941)

President Truman issued an executive order requiring fair employment in federal jobs (1948)

Supreme Court struck down segregated schools (   )

Black boycott of bus line in Montgomery, Alabama, marked first major attack on segregation of public facilities (1955-1956)

Civil Rights Acts passed (1954-1964, 1968)

Voting Rights Act passed (   )

Age Discrimination in Employment Act passed (1967)

Equal Employment Opportunities Act passed (1968)

Title IX of the Education Act banned discrimination on the basis of sex in educational programs that receive federal aid (1972)

Education for all Handicapped Children Act passed (1975)

Proposed equal rights amendment guaranteeing equal rights for women failed to be ratified (1982)

Equal Protection Timeline

1860

1870

1880

1890

1900

1910

1920

1930

1940

1950

1960

1970

1980

What is the right to due process and how is it protected?

LESSON OVERVIEW

The due process clause of the Fourteenth Amendment is considered one of the most important in the Constitution because it is the basis for many Supreme Court decisions limiting the authority of both federal and state governments. Due process can be divided into two types: (1) substantive due process, which deals with the fairness of the content of laws and (2) procedural due process, which deals with fair procedures for applying, interpreting, and enforcing the law.

The lesson opens with a discussion of the concept of fairness. Students then read a definition of due process and work in small groups to analyze a case study. Finally, students read and discuss the problem of balancing the rights of the individual with the rights of society.

LESSON OBJECTIVES

At the conclusion of this lesson:

1. Students should be able to give a general definition of due process and be able to distinguish between substantive and procedural due process.

2. Students should be able to explain the purpose of the due process clause in the Fourteenth Amendment in light of the fact that it was already included in the Fifth Amendment and additional procedural protection is included in several other amendments and in the body of the Constitution itself.

3. Students should be able to review the facts in a case, identify specific actions which they think are procedurally fair or unfair, and identify relevant provisions of the Constitution and Bill of Rights which may be applicable.

MATERIALS NEEDED

1. Student text

2. Handout 27-1 (optional)

TEACHING PROCEDURES

A. Introductory Activity:
Examining the concept of "fairness"

Write the word "fair" on the chalkboard. Have students suggest situations in which they think something fair or unfair has happened and briefly note these situations on the chalkboard. Inform students that "fairness" and "justice" mean pretty much the same thing. Then, present students the following three-part classification of issues of fairness and guide them in using it to classify the situations they have identified.

1. **Distributive fairness or justice** refers to the fairness of the distribution of the benefits and burdens in society, e.g., the fairness of the distribution of opportunities, pay, grades, responsibilities, taxes.

2. **Corrective fairness or justice** refers to the fairness of responses to wrongs or injuries, e.g., what "punishment fits the crime?" Is a punishment "cruel and unusual?"

3. **Procedural fairness or justice** refers to the fairness of the ways information is gathered and decisions are made, e.g., have people been tortured to gain information? Has a person been allowed to have a voice in a decision affecting him or her?

After classifying the situations students have identified, you might inform them that this lesson will deal with some of the most important parts of the Constitution that are designed to protect the people from unfair treatment by the state and federal governments.

B. Reading and Discussion:
Understanding due process

Have students read the "Purpose of Lesson" and the sections, "The due process clauses" and "What is due process of law?" Help students clarify their understanding of the difference between substantive and procedural due process. Also, be sure they understand how the due process clause of the Fourteenth Amendment has been used to make most of the Bill of Rights applicable to state governments.

C. Problem Solving:
Identifying issues of procedural due process

Divide the class into groups of from three to five students. Have each group read and complete the exercise described in the "Problem Solving" activity. Then, lead a class discussion of the groups' responses.

Note: The Supreme Court decided in the Gault case that juveniles are entitled to many of the same due process rights as adults, including the right to adequate written notice of the charges; to have an attorney, whether or not the defendant can afford to pay for one; to confront hostile witnesses, under oath; and to avoid self-incrimination.

D. Reading and Discussion:
Understanding the need to balance the rights of individuals with those of society

Have students read "The rights of the individual versus the rights of society." Discuss with them the importance of balancing the rights described and of the applicability of due process standards to the actions of all agencies of government, not just to the courts and law enforcement.

E. Concluding Activity

Conclude the lesson by leading a discussion of the questions included in "Reviewing and using the lesson." You may also wish to have students write an essay in their constitutional journals on the importance of due process for the protection of the rights of individuals.

OPTIONAL ACTIVITIES

For Reinforcement, Extended Learning, and Enrichment

1. Arrange to have the class visit and observe procedures at a local court hearing. If possible, have the judge discuss procedures with students.

2. Interested students might role play one or more of the hearings in the Gault case. They may wish to read some longer accounts of the case to gather additional information that will help them prepare for their roles.

3. Point out that the public gets much of its information about due process from television programs. Have students watch a television program about police work, taking notes on procedures followed. Then invite a police officer to visit the class and analyze the accuracy of the information conveyed on television.

4. Distribute Handout 27-1 and allow time for students to complete the worksheet. Students will need to use the Constitution provided in the "Reference Section" of the text to complete the exercise.

Due Process in the Constitution

Use the Constitution and the Bill of Rights to complete the chart below.

Due Process Rights	Where guaranteed in the Constitution
protection against unreasonable searches and seizures	
right to remain silent	
right to an attorney	
right to know the charges against oneself	
right to reasonable bail	
right to a trial by jury	
right to a public trial	
right to a speedy trial	
right to call witnesses in one's favor	
right to cross examine witnesses against oneself	
protection against cruel and unusual punishments	
protection against double jeopardy	

Unit Six

What are the responsibilities of citizens?

UNIT OVERVIEW

This concluding unit looks at the issues raised by the question, "What are the responsibilities of citizens?" Various forms of participation—including attending meetings, making contributions, writing letters, voting, campaigning, serving in public office, serving as a juror, among others—are discussed. The unit examines the relationship between rights and responsibilities, as well as the common welfare. The problem of what the citizen can do about unjust laws is also introduced. Throughout the discussion, students are reminded that the level and type of participation they undertake is a personal decision they must face.

UNIT OBJECTIVES

At the conclusion of this unit:

1. Students should be able to describe a variety of ways in which citizens participate in their government.

2. Students should be able to explain the advantages of participating in government.

3. Students should be able to take and defend a position on the responsibilities of citizenship, using ideas related to the common welfare.

How can citizens participate?

LESSON OVERVIEW

This lesson introduces the notion of citizen participation. It begins with students analyzing their own participation in the last school election. Then students read and discuss the definition of the term "citizen." Students take part in a problem-solving activity in which they learn of various forms of political participation and they identify and discuss their advantages and disadvantages. The lesson ends with a discussion of why citizens should participate and what factors they should consider in making decisions about participation.

LESSON OBJECTIVES

At the conclusion of this lesson:

1. Students should be able to describe the characteristics of a citizen.

2. Students should be able to list various ways that citizens can participate in government.

3. Students should be able to develop and support positions on why and how much a citizen should participate.

4. Students should be able to explain how participation is related to the purpose of our constitutional government.

MATERIALS NEEDED

1. Student text

2. Handouts 28-1 and 28-2 (optional)

TEACHING PROCEDURES

A. Introductory Activity:
Analyzing participation

1. Have students look through newspapers or newsmagazines for evidence of citizen participation. Based on their findings, compile a class list of ways to participate in government. Post this list on the board and tell students that they can add to it as they learn more about participation. At the end of the unit, they will use the list to make a class bulletin board display on participation.

2. This activity calls upon students to examine their own participation in the most recent school election. Distribute copies of Handout 28-1 and allow time for students to complete the worksheet. (Alternatively, you might write the questions on the chalkboard.) Collect the worksheets and have a small group of students tally the results and prepare a report for the class.

Use the following questions to analyze the results of the survey:

- How many members of the class participated in the last election? How many did not?
- What reasons did individuals have for participating? For not participating?
- What effect did participation have on those who worked for candidates? On those who voted? On those who did not?
- Would the outcome be different if the nonparticipants had voted? Should citizens be forced to vote?
- Based on this discussion, will you participate any differently in the next school election? Why?
- Do you expect that your role in school elections is similar or different from the role you will take in governmental elections when you turn 18? (Explain that citizens aged 18 to 24 are among the least likely to vote.)
- How does low voter turnout affect the political power of young people?

B. Reading and discussion:
Defining "citizen"

Have students read the "Purpose of Lesson" and "Who is a citizen?" Be sure they understand that the difference between citizens and aliens is that citizens can participate in the political system and aliens can't.

C. Reading and Problem Solving:
Identifying and analyzing forms of participation

Divide the class into groups of three to five students and have them complete the "Problem Solving" exercise. Then, have groups report on their findings and have the class discuss them.

D. Reading and Discussion:
Deciding upon participation

Write the following question on the board, "How satisfied are you with our government?" Have students pick a number between 1 and 10 to describe their level of satisfaction and explain their answer by listing five things that support their level of satisfaction or dissatisfaction.

Then have students read "Should citizens participate?" Be sure students understand the analogy of the bicycle repairperson. Then, ask students to evaluate and revise their initial responses to the above question based on their level of satisfaction with the government and the information in the reading. Discuss these reassessments. Then, place the following two headings on the chalkboard: "How students can participate?" and "Should students participate?" Have students suggest responses for each heading and discuss these responses in light of the principles and values of constitutional democracy they have studied.

E. Concluding Activity

Conclude the lesson by leading a class discussion of the questions contained in "Reviewing and using the lesson." Then, have students write answers to the following question in their constitutional journals: "If Abigail Adams (or another Founder) were alive today, in what forms of participation do you think she would be involved? Explain your answer."

OPTIONAL ACTIVITIES

For Reinforcement, Extended Learning, and Enrichment

1. Have students read the editorials and letters to the editor in the local newspaper to identify issues about which people in your community seem to be dissatisfied. Students could then design a citizen participation campaign to achieve the desired change or improvement.

2. Have students look in their collection of articles and pictures depicting participation to see how many of the kinds of participation are illustrated. They should search other sources for stories or pictures illustrating those that are not yet represented. Their goal should be to have all the ways of participation covered by the time they do the bulletin board project.

3. Divide the class into groups of three to five students and provide them with copies of Handout 28-2. (Alternatively, you could list the questions on the chalkboard.) Each group should examine, analyze, and discuss the list to determine:

   - Which items are most important for our society?
   - Are all items equally important?
   - What would happen if no one did these things?

   Next, have students check the forms of participation they would most likely do. Possible discussion questions are:

   - Are some people interested and willing to participate in each of the ways?
   - How much time will be needed to complete the tasks they have checked?
   - How much time do you think you need to spend on being a citizen?
   - In which categories are they as a group the weakest? The strongest?

Participation in School Elections

Think back to the last school election in which you had an opportunity to participate. Which of the following represents you?

_____ 1. I voted.

_____ 2. I ran for office.

_____ 3. I signed a petition to nominate someone.

_____ 4. I wrote a speech for myself or for a friend.

_____ 5. I wore a campaign button.

_____ 6. I distributed materials.

_____ 7. I made posters.

_____ 8. I contributed money.

_____ 9. Other. Explain.

_____10. I did nothing.

How much time did you spend on these activities?

What reasons did you have for your choice(s)?

After the election, how did you feel about your level of participation?

Citizen Participation Checklist

In the first column after each item below, place an I if you think the item is important. In the second column, place an M by items you would be likely to do. In the third column, estimate the time you would spend each week doing the activity.

Form of participation	Rating importance	Likely to do?	How much time?
Keeping informed.			
Voting in local, state, and national elections.			
Initiating a political discussion.			
Trying to persuade someone to vote a certain way.			
Signing a petition.			
Wearing a button or putting a sticker on the car.			
Writing letters to elected representatives.			
Contributing money to a party or candidate.			
Attending meetings to gain information, discuss issues, or lend support.			
Campaigning for a candidate.			
Lobbying for laws that are of special interest.			
Demonstrating through boycotts, parades, sit-ins, or other forms of protest.			
Serving as a juror.			
Running for office.			
Holding public office.			
Serving the country through the military or other service.			
Disobeying laws and paying the consequences.			

Lesson 29

What decisions will you make as a citizen?

LESSON OVERVIEW

This final lesson looks at three important questions that students will face as citizens:

- What responsibilities accompany our basic rights?
- Must you obey a law you think is unjust?
- What is the common welfare?

The lesson begins with a class discussion of the responsibilities accompanying our basic rights. Students then study the dilemma of what to do when a law conflicts with what a citizen thinks is right or just. Students read about the difficulty of defining the common welfare and take part in a problem-solving activity which calls for them to consider a situation in which a representative faces conflicting responsibilities. The lesson concludes with the question of what are the responsibilities of the citizen.

LESSON OBJECTIVES

At the conclusion of this lesson:

1. Students should be able to explain three responsibilities that accompany basic rights.

2. Students should be able to explain why people sometimes choose to disobey a law and the consequences of such actions.

3. Students should be able to describe why it is sometimes difficult to agree upon what is best for the common welfare.

MATERIALS NEEDED

1. Student text

2. Handout 29-1 (optional)

TEACHING PROCEDURES

A. Reading and Discussion:
Identifying the responsibilities accompanying rights

Have the class read the "Purpose of Lesson" and "What responsibilities accompany our basic rights?" Lead the class in a discussion of the following questions:

- What basic rights and responsibilities that accompany them would you add to those described in the text?
- Do the responsibilities described in the text and any additional responsibilities you have identified seem fair and just? Why or why not?
- Are the responsibilities communicated effectively to all members of our society?
- How do young children learn these responsibilities?

- Which responsibilities do we as citizens have the most difficulty fulfilling?
- Which ones do we expect most often of each other?
- How would the responsibilities of citizenship differ if you lived under a dictatorship?

B. Problem Solving:
Dealing with laws thought to be unjust

Have students read the section, "Must you obey a law you think is unjust?" Discuss the examples provided in the text. Then, divide the class into groups of three to five students and introduce the "Problem Solving" exercise. Make sure students understand the decision-making steps provided. Allow time for the groups to work through Mark's dilemma, using the steps suggested. You may wish to provide poster paper and markers, or use the chalkboard, so the groups can list the alternatives, their advantages and disadvantages, and the group's decision in large enough lettering for presentation to the class.

Conclude the activity by having the groups discuss their decisions.

C. Reading and Discussion:
Identifying the common welfare

Have the class read the section entitled "What is the common welfare?" Place the information on Hand-out 29-1 on the chalkboard or distribute copies of the handout and allow time for students to complete the worksheet. Ask students whether completing the worksheet helped or hindered them in the task of defining the common welfare. Discuss their responses to the examples provided on the worksheet.

D. Problem Solving:
Understanding conflicting responsibilities of representatives

Have students read "Conflicting responsibilities of a representative" in the second "Problem Solving" activity. Divide the class into groups of three to five students and have each group develop its own answers to the questions in the exercise. Then have the groups report their findings to the entire class for further discussion.

E. Concluding Activity

Have students read "What are your responsibilities as a citizen?" Discuss the questions asked in "Reviewing and using the lesson." You may also wish to have students write their thoughts about what they have learned from the text and class discussions in their constitutional journals.

OPTIONAL ACTIVITIES

For Reinforcement, Extended Learning, and Enrichment

1. Have students complete their bulletin board project. The bulletin board should include examples of all the kinds of participation discussed in the unit. Students might also want to devote a portion of the bulletin board to defining the common welfare.

2. Have students write reports on people who practiced civil disobedience and how they dealt with the consequences of their actions.

3. Ask each student to identify one idea from this unit that they think will be helpful to them in making decisions as citizens. Each student should make a poster depicting the idea selected. You may wish to display the posters where other classes can see them.

4. Have students write a short essay in which they describe the qualities of the good citizen. They should explain why they think those qualities are necessary. They should also consider whether or not different kinds of political systems might not need different kinds of good citizens.

5. "Gandhi" and "Cry Freedom" are two recent movies on videotape that might be considered for viewing. Also, the PBS series, "Eyes on the Prize" might be an excellent way to supplement the ideas about citizens and unjust laws.

Defining the Common Welfare

For each of the possible actions below, check whether it would be in your personal interest, the interest of your family and friends, and the interest of most other Americans. In the last column, mark whether the action promotes the common welfare.

Possible action	My Interest	Interest of family and friends	Interest of most other Americans	Common welfare
High fees for families of students in public schools to provide more teachers				
Mandatory public service (either military or civilian) for all young people aged 18-20				
Increase in state income taxes to pay for aid to the homeless				
Cuts in aid to developing nations				
Mandatory drug testing of junior high and high school students				

Reference Section

Declaration of Independence

IN CONGRESS, JULY 4, 1776.

A DECLARATION

BY THE REPRESENTATIVES OF THE

UNITED STATES OF AMERICA,

IN GENERAL CONGRESS ASSEMBLED

WHEN in the Course of human Events, it becomes necessary for one People to dissolve the Political Bands which have connected them with another, and to assume among the Powers of the Earth, the separate and equal Station to which the Laws of Nature and of Nature's God entitle them, a decent Respect to the Opinions of Mankind requires that they should declare the causes which impel them to the Separation.

We hold these Truths to be self-evident, that all Men are created equal, that they are endowed by their Creator with certain unalienable Rights, that among these are Life, Liberty, and the Pursuit of Happiness-- That to secure these Rights, Governments are instituted among Men, deriving their just Powers from the Consent of the Governed, that whenever any Form of Government becomes destructive of these Ends it is the Right of the People to alter or to abolish it, and to institute new Government, laying its Foundation on such Principles, and organizing its Powers in such Form, as to them shall seem most likely to effect their Safety and Happiness. Prudence, indeed, will dictate that Governments long established should not be changed for light and transient Causes; and accordingly all Experience hath shewn, that Mankind are more disposed to suffer, while Evils are sufferable, than to right themselves by abolishing the Forms to which they are accustomed. But when a long Train of Abuses and Usurpations, pursuing invariably the same Object, evinces a Design to reduce them under absolute Despotism, it is their Right, it is their Duty, to throw off such Government, and to provide new Guards for their future Security. Such has been the patient Sufferance of these Colonies; and such is now the Necessity which constrains them to alter their former Systems of Government. The History of the present King of Great-Britain is a History of repeated Injuries and Usurpations, all having in direct Object the Establishment of an absolute Tyranny over these States. To prove this, let Facts be submitted to a candid World.

He has refused his Assent to Laws, the most wholesome and necessary for the public Good.

He has forbidden his Governors to pass Laws of immediate and pressing Importance, unless suspended in their Operation till his Assent should be obtained; and when so suspended, he has utterly neglected to attend to them.

He has refused to pass other Laws for the Accommodation of large Districts of People, unless those People would relinquish the Right of Representation in the Legislature, a Right inestimable to them, and formidable to Tyrants only.

He has called together Legislative Bodies at Places unusual, uncomfortable, and distant from the Depository of their public Records, for the sole Purpose of fatiguing them into Compliance with his Measures.

He has dissolved Representative Houses repeatedly, for opposing with manly Firmness his Invasions on the Rights of the People.

He has refused for a long Time, after such Dissolutions, to cause others to be elected; whereby the Legislative Powers, incapable of Annihilation, have returned to the People at large for their exercise; the State remaining in the mean time exposed to all the Dangers of Invasions from without, and Convulsions within.

He has endeavored to prevent the Population of these States; for that Purpose obstructing the Laws for Naturalization of Foreigners; refusing to pass others to encourage their Migrations hither, and raising the Conditions of new Appropriations of Lands.

He has obstructed the Administration of Justice, by refusing his Assent to Laws for establishing Judiciary Powers.

He has made Judges dependent on his Will alone, for the Tenure of their Offices, and the Amount and Payment of their Salaries.

He has erected a Multitude of new Offices, and sent hither Swarms of Officers to harass our People and eat out their Substance.

He has kept among us, in Times of Peace, Standing Armies, without the consent of our Legislatures.

He has affected to render the Military independent of and superior to the Civil Power.

He has combined with others to subject us to a Jurisdiction foreign to our Constitution, and unacknowledged by our Laws; giving his Assent to their Acts of pretended Legislation:

For quartering large Bodies of Armed Troops among us:

For protecting them, by a mock Trial, from Punishment for any Murders which they should commit on the Inhabitants of these States:

For cutting off our Trade with all Parts of the World:

For imposing Taxes on us without our Consent:

For depriving us, in many Cases, of the Benefits of Trial by Jury:

For transporting us beyond Seas to be tried for pretended Offenses:

For abolishing the free System of English Laws in a neighbouring Province, establishing therein an Arbitrary Government, and enlarging its Boundaries, so as to render it at once an Example and fit Instrument for introducing the same absolute Rule into these Colonies:

For taking away our Charters, abolishing our most valuable Laws, and altering fundamentally the Forms of our Governments:

For suspending our own Legislatures, and declaring themselves invested with Power to legislate for us in all Cases whatsoever.

He has abdicated Government here, by declaring us out of his Protection and waging War against us.

He has plundered our Seas, ravaged our Coasts, burnt our Towns, and destroyed the Lives of our People.

He is, at this Time, transporting large Armies of foreign Mercenaries to compleat the Works of Death, Desolation, and Tyranny, already begun with circumstances of Cruelty and Perfidy, scarcely paralleled in the most barbarous Ages, and totally unworthy the Head of a civilized Nation.

He has constrained our fellow Citizens taken Captive on the high Seas to bear Arms against their Country, to become the Executioners of their Friends and Brethren, or to fall themselves by their Hands.

He has excited domestic Insurrections amongst us, and has endeavoured to bring on the Inhabitants of our Frontiers, the merciless Indian Savages, whose known Rule of Warfare, is an undistinguished Destruction, of all Ages, Sexes and Conditions.

In every stage of these Oppressions we have Petitioned for Redress in the most humble Terms: Our repeated Petitions have been answered only by repeated Injury. A Prince, whose Character is thus marked by every act which may define a Tyrant, is unfit to be the Ruler of a free People.

Nor have we been wanting in Attentions to our British Brethren. We have warned them from Time to Time of Attempts by their Legislature to extend an unwarrantable Jurisdiction over us. We have reminded them of the Circumstances of our Emigration and Settlement here. We have appealed to their native Justice and Magnanimity, and we have conjured them by the Ties of our common Kindred to disavow these Usurpations, which, would inevitably interrupt our Connections and Correspondence. They too have been deaf to the Voice of Justice and of Consanguinity. We must, therefore, acquiesce in the Necessity, which denounces our Separation, and hold them, as we hold the rest of Mankind, Enemies in War, in Peace, Friends.

We, therefore, the Representatives of the UNITED STATES OF AMERICA, in GENERAL CONGRESS, Assembled, appealing to the Supreme Judge of the World for the Rectitude of our Intentions, do, in the Name, and by Authority of the good People of these Colonies, solemnly Publish and Declare, That these United Colonies are, and of Right ought to be, FREE AND INDEPENDENT STATES; that they are absolved from all Allegiance to the British Crown, and that all political Connection between them and the State of Great-Britain, is and ought to be totally dissolved; and that as FREE AND INDEPENDENT STATES, they have full Power to levy War, conclude Peace, contract Alliances, establish Commerce, and to do all other Acts and Things which INDEPENDENT STATES may of right do. And for the support of this Declaration, with a firm Reliance on the Protection of divine Providence, we mutually pledge to each other our Lives, our Fortunes, and our sacred Honor.

Signed by ORDER and in BEHALF of the CONGRESS,

JOHN HANCOCK, PRESIDENT.

Signers of the Declaration of Independence

New-Hampshire
Josiah Bartlett,
Wm. Whipple,
Matthew Thornton.

Massachusetts-Bay.
Saml. Adams,
John Adams,
Robt. Treat Paine,
Elbridge Gerry.

Rhode-Island and Providence, &c.
Step. Hopkins,
William Ellery.

Connecticut.
Roger Sherman,
Saml. Huntington,
Wm. Williams,
Oliver Wolcott.

New-York
Wm. Floyd,
Phil. Livingston,
Frans. Lewis,
Lewis Morris.

New-Jersey
Richd. Stockton,
Jno. Witherspoon,
Fras. Hopkinson,
John Hart,
Abra. Clark.

Pennsylvania
Robt. Morris,
Benjamin Rush,
Benja. Franklin,
John Morton,
Geo. Clymer,
Jas. Smith
Geo. Taylor,
James Wilson,
Geo. Ross.

Delaware
Casar Rodney,
Geo. Read,
(Tho M:Kean.)

Maryland
Samuel Chase,
Wm. Paca,
Thos. Stone,
Charles Carroll, of Carrollton.

Virginia
George Wythe,
Richard Henry Lee,
Ths. Jefferson,
Benja. Harrison,
Thos. Nelson, jr.
Francis Lightfoot Lee,
Carter Braxton.

North-Carolina.
Wm. Hooper
Joseph Hewes,
John Penn.

South-Carolina.
Edward Rutledge,
Thos. Heyward, junr.
Thomas Lynch, junr.
Arthur Middleton.

Georgia.
Button Gwinnett,
Lyman Hall,
Geo. Walton.

According to the authenticated list printed by order of Congress of January 18, 1777.
Spelling and abbreviations of names conform to original printed list.

The Constitution of the United States of America

Preamble

We the People of the United States, in Order to form a more perfect Union, establish Justice, insure domestic tranquility, provide for the common defence, promote the general Welfare, and secure the Blessings of Liberty to ourselves and our Posterity, do ordain and establish this Constitution for the United States of America.

ARTICLE I.

The Legislative Branch

Section 1.

All legislative Powers herein granted shall be vested in a Congress of the United States, which shall consist of a Senate and House of Representatives.

Section 2.

House of Representatives: Organization and Power of Impeachment

1. The House of Representatives shall be composed of Members chosen every second Year by the People of the several States, and the Electors in each State shall have the Qualifications requisite for Electors of the most numerous Branch of the State Legislature.

2. No Person shall be a Representative who shall not have attained to the Age of twenty five Years, and been seven Years a Citizen of the United States, and who shall not, when elected, be an Inhabitant of that State in which he shall be chosen.

3. [Representatives and direct Taxes shall be apportioned among the several States which may be included within this Union, according to their respective Numbers, which shall be determined by adding to the whole Number of free Persons, including those bound to Service for a Term of Years, and excluding Indians not taxed, three fifths of all other Persons.]* The actual Enumeration shall be made within three Years after the first Meeting of the Congress of the United States, and within every subsequent Term of ten Years, in such Manner as they shall by Law direct. The number of Representatives shall not exceed one for every thirty Thousand, but each State shall have at Least one Representative; and until such enumeration shall be made, the State of New Hampshire shall be entitled to choose three, Massachusetts eight, Rhode Island and Providence Plantations one, Connecticut five, New York six, New Jersey four, Pennsylvania eight, Delaware one, Maryland six, Virginia ten, North Carolina five, South Carolina five, and Georgia three.

4. When vacancies happen in the Representation from any State, the Executive Authority thereof shall issue Writs of Election to fill such Vacancies.

5. The House of Representatives shall choose their Speaker and other Officers; and shall have the sole Power of Impeachment.

Section 3.

The Senate, Organization and Powers of Impeachment

1. The Senate of the United States shall be composed of two Senators from each State, [chosen by the Legislature thereof,]** for six Years; and each Senator shall have one Vote.

2. Immediately after they shall be assembled in Consequence of the first Election, they shall be divided as equally as may be into three Classes. The seats of the Senators of the first Class shall be vacated at the Expiration of the second Year, of the second Class at the Expiration of the fourth Year, and of the third Class at the Expiration of the sixth Year, so that one third may be chosen every second Year; [and if Vacancies happen by Resignation, or otherwise, during the Recess of the Legislature of any State, the Executive thereof may make temporary Appointments until the next Meeting of the Legislature, which shall then fill such Vacancies.]**

3. No Person shall be a Senator who shall not have attained to the Age of thirty Years, and been nine Years a Citizen of the United States, and who shall not, when elected, be an Inhabitant of that State for which he shall be chosen.

4. The Vice President of the United States shall be President of the Senate, but shall have no Vote, unless they be equally divided.

5. The Senate shall choose their other officers, and also a President pro tempore, in the Absence of

*Changed by section 2 of the Fourteenth Amendment.

**Changed by the Seventeenth Amendment.

the Vice President, or when he shall exercise the Office of President of the United States.

6. The Senate shall have the sole Power to try all Impeachments. When sitting for that Purpose, they shall be on Oath or Affirmation. When the President of the United States is tried, the Chief Justice shall preside: And no person shall be convicted without the Concurrence of two thirds of the Members present.

7. Judgment in Cases of Impeachment shall not extend further than to removal from Office, and disqualification to hold and enjoy any Office of honor, Trust or Profit under the United States; but the Party convicted shall nevertheless be liable and subject to Indictment, Trial, Judgment and Punishment, according to Law.

Section 4.
Elections and Meeting of Congress

1. The Times, Places and Manner of holding Elections for Senators and Representatives shall be prescribed in each State by the Legislature thereof; but the Congress may at any time by Law make or alter such Regulations, except as to the Places of choosing Senators.

2. The Congress shall assemble at least once in every Year, and such Meeting shall be [on the first Monday in December,]* unless they shall by Law appoint a different Day.

Section 5.
Congress's Rules of Procedure, Powers, Quorum, Journals, Meetings, Adjournments

1. Each House shall be the Judge of the Elections, Returns and Qualifications of its own Members, and a Majority of each shall constitute a Quorum to do Business; but a smaller Number may adjourn from day to day, and may be authorized to compel the Attendance of absent Members, in such Manner, and under such Penalties as each House may provide.

2. Each House may determine the Rules of its Proceedings, punish its members for disorderly Behavior, and, with the Concurrence of two thirds, expel a Member.

3. Each House shall keep a Journal of its Proceedings, and from time to time publish the same, excepting such Parts as may in their Judgment require Secrecy; and the Yeas and Nays of the Members of either House on any question shall, at

the Desire of one fifth of those Present, be entered on the Journal.

4. Neither House, during the Session of Congress, shall, without the Consent of the other, adjourn for more than three days, nor to any other Place than that in which the two Houses shall be sitting.

Section 6.
Pay, Privileges, Limitations

1. The Senators and Representatives shall receive a Compensation for their Services, to be ascertained by Law, and paid out of the Treasury of the United States. They shall in all cases, except Treason, Felony and Breach of the Peace, be privileged from Arrest during their Attendance at the Session of their respective Houses, and in going to and returning from the same; and for any Speech or Debate in either House, they shall not be questioned in any other Place.

2. No Senator or Representative shall, during the Time for which he was elected, be appointed to any civil Office under the Authority of the United States, which shall have been created, or the Emoluments whereof shall have been increased during such time; and no Person holding any Office under the United States, shall be a Member of either House during his Continuance in Office.

Section 7.
Procedure in Passing Bills, President's Veto Power

1. All Bills for raising Revenue shall originate in the House of Representatives; but the Senate may propose or concur with Amendments as on other Bills.

2. Every Bill which shall have passed the House of Representatives and the Senate, shall, before it becomes a Law, be presented to the President of the United States; if he approve he shall sign it, but if not he shall return it, with his Objections, to that House in which it shall have originated, who shall enter the Objections at large on their Journal, and proceed to reconsider it. If after such Reconsideration two thirds of that House shall agree to pass the Bill, it shall be sent, together with the Objections, to the other House, by which it shall likewise be reconsidered, and if approved by two thirds of that House, it shall become a Law. But in all such Cases the Votes of both Houses shall be determined by yeas and nays, and the Names of the Persons voting for and against the Bill shall be

*Changed by section 2 of the Twentieth Amendment.

entered on the Journal of each House respectively. If any Bill shall not be returned by the President within ten Days (Sundays excepted) after it shall have been presented to him, the Same shall be a Law, in like Manner as if he had signed it, unless the Congress by their Adjournment prevent its Return, in which Case it shall not be a Law.

3. Every Order, Resolution, or Vote to which the Concurrence of the Senate and House of Representatives may be necessary (except on a question of Adjournment) shall be presented to the President of the United States; and before the Same shall take Effect, shall be approved by him, or being disapproved by him, shall be repassed by two thirds of the Senate and House of Representatives, according to the Rules and Limitations prescribed in the Case of a Bill.

Section 8.
Powers Delegated to Congress

The Congress shall have Power

1. To lay and collect Taxes, Duties, Imposts and Excises, to pay the Debts and provide for the common Defence and general Welfare of the United States; but all Duties, Imposts and Excises shall be uniform throughout the United States;

2. To borrow Money on the credit of the United States;

3. To regulate Commerce with foreign Nations, and among the several States, and with the Indian Tribes;

4. To establish an uniform Rule of Naturalization, and uniform Laws on the subject of Bankruptcies throughout the United States;

5. To coin Money, regulate the Value thereof, and of Foreign Coin, and fix the Standard of Weights and Measures;

6. To provide for the Punishment of counterfeiting the Securities and current Coin of the United States;

7. To establish Post Offices and post Roads;

8. To promote the Progress of Science and useful Arts, by securing for limited Times to Authors and Inventors the exclusive Right to their respective Writings and Discoveries;

9. To constitute Tribunals inferior to the supreme Court;

10. To define and punish Piracies and Felonies committed on the high Seas, and Offenses against the Law of Nations;

11. To declare War, grant Letters of Marque and Reprisal, and make Rules concerning Captures on Land and Water;

12. To raise and support Armies, but no Appropriation of Money to that Use shall be for a longer Term than two Years;

13. To provide and maintain a Navy;

14. To make Rules for the Government and Regulation of the land and naval Forces;

15. To provide for calling forth the Militia to execute the Laws of the Union, suppress Insurrections and repel Invasions;

16. To provide for organizing, arming, and disciplining the Militia, and for governing such Part of them as may be employed in the Service of the United States, reserving to the States respectively, the Appointment of the Officers, and the Authority of training the Militia according to the discipline prescribed by Congress;

17. To exercise exclusive Legislation in all Cases whatsoever, over such District (not exceeding ten Miles square) as may, by Cession of particular States, and the Acceptance of Congress, become the Seat of the Government of the United States, and to exercise like Authority over all Places purchased by the Consent of the Legislature of the State in which the Same shall be, for the Erection of Forts, Magazines, Arsenals, dock-Yards and other needful Buildings;— And

18. To make all Laws which shall be necessary and proper for carrying into Execution the foregoing powers, and all other Powers vested by this Constitution in the Government of the United States, or in any Department or Officer thereof.

Section 9.
Powers Denied to Congress

1. The Migration or Importation of such Persons as any of the States now existing shall think proper to admit, shall not be prohibited by the Congress prior to the Year one thousand eight hundred and eight, but a Tax or duty may be imposed on such Importation, not exceeding ten dollars for each Person.

2. The Privilege of the Writ of Habeas Corpus shall not be suspended, unless when in Cases of

Rebellion or Invasion the public Safety may require it.

3. No Bill of Attainder or ex post facto Law shall be passed.

4. [No Capitation, or other direct, Tax shall be laid, unless in Proportion to the Census or Enumeration herein before directed to be taken.]*

5. No Tax or Duty shall be laid on Articles exported from any State.

6. No Preference shall be given by any Regulation of Commerce or Revenue to the Ports of one State over those of another: nor shall Vessels bound to, or from, one State, be obliged to enter, clear, or pay Duties in another.

7. No Money shall be drawn from the Treasury, but in Consequence of Appropriations made by Law; and a regular Statement and Account of the Receipts and Expenditures of all public Money shall be published from time to time.

8. No Title of Nobility shall be granted by the United States: And no Person holding any Office of Profit or Trust under them, shall, without the Consent of the Congress, accept of any present, Emolument, Office, or Title, of any kind whatever, from any King, Prince, or foreign State.

Section 10.

Restrictions on States' Powers

1. No State shall enter into any Treaty, Alliance, or Confederation; grant Letters of Marque and Reprisal; coin Money; emit Bills of Credit; make any Thing but gold and silver Coin a Tender in Payment of Debts; pass any Bill of Attainder, ex post facto Law, or Law impairing the Obligation of Contracts, or grant any Title of Nobility.

2. No State shall, without the Consent of the Congress, lay any Imposts or Duties on Imports or Exports, except what may be absolutely necessary for executing its inspection Laws: and the net Produce of all Duties and Imposts, laid by any State on Imports or Exports, shall be for the Use of the Treasury of the United States; and all such Laws shall be subject to the Revision and Control of the Congress.

3. No State shall, without the Consent of Congress, lay any Duty of Tonnage, keep Troops, or Ships of War in time of Peace, enter into any Agreement or Compact with another State, or with a foreign Power, or engage in War, unless actually

invaded, or in such imminent Danger as will not admit of delay.

ARTICLE II.

The Executive Branch

Section 1.

President and Vice-President: Election, Qualifications, and Oath

1. The executive Power shall be vested in a President of the United States of America. He shall hold his Office during the term of four Years, and, together with the Vice President, chosen for the same Term, be elected, as follows.

2. Each State shall appoint, in such Manner as the Legislature thereof may direct, a Number of Electors, equal to the whole Number of Senators and Representatives to which the State may be entitled in the Congress: but no Senator or Representative, or Person holding an Office of Trust or Profit under the United States, shall be appointed an Elector.

3. [The Electors shall meet in their respective states, and vote by Ballot for two Persons, of whom one at least shall not be an Inhabitant of the same State with themselves. And they shall make a List of all the Persons voted for, and of the Number of Votes for each; which List they shall sign and certify, and transmit sealed to the Seat of the Government of the United States, directed to the President of the Senate. The President of the Senate shall, in the Presence of the Senate and House of Representatives, open all the Certificates, and the Votes shall then be counted. The Person having the greatest Number of Votes shall be the President, if such Number be a Majority of the whole Number of Electors appointed; and if there be more than one who have such Majority, and have an equal Number of Votes, then the House of Representatives shall immediately choose by Ballot one of them for President; and if no Person have a Majority, then from the five highest on the List the said House shall in like manner choose the President. But in choosing the President, the Votes shall be taken by States, the Representation from each State having one Vote; A quorum for this Purpose shall consist of a Member or Members from two thirds of the States, and a Majority of all the States shall be necessary to a Choice. In every Case, after the Choice of the President, the Person having the greatest Number of Votes of the Electors shall be the Vice President. But if there should remain two or more who have

*Changed by the Sixteenth Amendment.

equal Votes, the Senate shall choose from them by Ballot the Vice President.]*

4. The Congress may determine the Time of choosing the Electors, and the day on which they shall give their Votes; which Day shall be the same throughout the United States.

5. No Person except a natural born Citizen, or a Citizen of the United States at the time of the Adoption of this Constitution, shall be eligible to the Office of the President; neither shall any person be eligible to that Office who shall not have attained to the Age of thirty five Years, and been fourteen Years a Resident within the United States.

6. [In Case of the Removal of the President from Office, or of his Death, Resignation, or Inability to discharge the Powers and Duties of the said Office, the Same shall devolve on the Vice President, and the Congress may by Law provide for the Case of Removal, Death, Resignation or Inability, both of the President and Vice President, declaring what Officer shall then act as President, and such Officer shall act accordingly, until the Disability be removed, or a President shall be elected.]**

7. The President shall, at stated Times, receive for his Services, a Compensation, which shall neither be increased nor diminished during the Period for which he shall have been elected, and he shall not receive within that Period any other Emolument from the United States, or any of them.

8. Before he enter the Execution of his Office, he shall take the following Oath or Affirmation: — "I do solemnly swear (or affirm) that I will faithfully execute the Office of President of the United States, and will to the best of my Ability, preserve, protect, and defend the Constitution of the United States."

Section 2.
Powers of the President

1. The President shall be Commander in Chief of the Army and Navy of the United States, and of the Militia of the several States, when called into the actual Service of the United States; he may require the Opinion, in writing, of the principal Officer in each of the executive Departments, upon any Subject relating to the Duties of their respective Offices, and he shall have Power to grant Reprieves and Pardons for Offenses against the United States, except in Cases of Impeachment.

2. He shall have Power, by and with the Advice and Consent of the Senate, to make Treaties, provided two thirds of the Senators present concur; and he shall nominate, and by and with the Advice and Consent of the Senate, shall appoint Ambassadors, other public Ministers and Consuls, Judges of the supreme Court, and all other Officers of the United States, whose Appointments are not herein otherwise provided for, and which shall be established by Law: but the Congress may by Law vest the Appointment of such inferior Officers, as they think proper, in the President alone, in the Courts of Law, or in the Heads of Departments.

3. The President shall have Power to fill up all Vacancies that may happen during the Recess of the Senate, by granting Commissions which shall expire at the End of their next Session.

Section 3.
Duties of the President

He shall from time to time give to the Congress Information of the State of the Union, and recommend to their Consideration such Measures as he shall judge necessary and expedient; he may, on extraordinary Occasions, convene both Houses, or either of them, and in Case of Disagreement between them, with Respect to the Time of Adjournment, he may adjourn them to such Time as he shall think proper; he shall receive Ambassadors and other public Ministers; he shall take Care that the Laws be faithfully executed, and shall Commission all the Officers of the United States.

Section 4.
Impeachment and Removal from Office for Crimes

The President, Vice President and all civil Officers of the United States, shall be removed from Office on Impeachment for, and Conviction of, Treason, Bribery, or other high Crimes and Misdemeanors.

ARTICLE III.
The Judicial Branch

Section 1.
Federal Courts, Tenure of Office

The judicial Power of the United States, shall be vested in one supreme Court, and in such inferior Courts as the Congress may from time to time ordain and establish. The Judges, both of the supreme and inferior Courts, shall hold their Offices during good Behavior, and shall, at stated

*Changed by the Twelfth Amendment.
**Changed by the Twenty-Fifth Amendment.

Times, receive for their Services a Compensation, which shall not be diminished during their Continuance in Office.

Section 2.
Jurisdiction of Federal Courts

1. The judicial Power shall extend to all Cases, in Law and Equity, arising under this Constitution, the Laws of the United States, and Treaties made, or which shall be made, under their Authority;— to all Cases affecting Ambassadors, other public Ministers and Consuls;— to all Cases of admiralty and maritime Jurisdiction;— to Controversies to which the United States shall be a Party;— to Controversies between two or more States; [between a State and Citizens of another State;]* between Citizens of different States;—between Citizens of the same State claiming Lands under Grants of different States;—[and between a State, or the Citizens thereof, and foreign States, Citizens or Subjects.]*

2. In all Cases affecting Ambassadors, other public Ministers and Consuls, and those in which a State shall be Party, the supreme Court shall have original Jurisdiction. In all the other Cases before mentioned, the supreme Court shall have appellate Jurisdiction, both as to Law and Fact, with such Exceptions, and under such Regulations as the Congress shall make.

3. The Trial of all Crimes, except in Cases of Impeachment, shall be by Jury; and such Trial shall be held in the State where said Crimes shall have been committed; but when not committed within any State, the Trial shall be at such Place or Places as the Congress may by Law have directed.

Section 3.
Treason: Conviction Of and Punishment For

1. Treason against the United States shall consist only in levying War against them, or in adhering to their Enemies, giving them Aid and Comfort. No Person shall be convicted of Treason unless on the Testimony of two Witnesses to the same overt Act, or on Confession in open Court.

2. The Congress shall have Power to declare the Punishment of Treason, but no Attainder of Treason shall work Corruption of Blood, or Forfeiture except during the Life of the Person attainted.

ARTICLE IV.
Relations Among the States
Section 1.
Full Faith and Credit

Full Faith and Credit shall be given in each State to the public Acts, Records, and judicial Proceedings of every other State; And the Congress may by general Laws prescribe the manner in which such Acts, Records and Proceedings shall be proved, and the Effect thereof.

Section 2.
Rights of State Citizens; Right of Extradition

1. The Citizens of each State shall be entitled to all Privileges and Immunities of Citizens in the several States.

2. A Person charged in any State with Treason, Felony, or other Crime, who shall flee from Justice, and be found in another State, shall on Demand of the executive Authority of the State from which he fled, be delivered up, to be removed to the State having Jurisdiction of the Crime.

3. [No person held to Service or Labour in one State, under the Laws thereof, escaping into another, shall, in Consequence of any Law or Regulation therein, be discharged from such Service or Labour, but shall be delivered up on Claim of the Party to whom such Service or Labour may be due.]* **

Section 3.
Admission of New States

1. New States may be admitted by the Congress into this Union; but no new State shall be formed or erected within the Jurisdiction of any other State; nor any State be formed by the Junction of two or more States, or parts of States, without the Consent of the Legislatures of the States concerned as well as of the Congress.

2. The Congress shall have Power to dispose of and make all needful Rules and Regulations respecting the territory or other Property belonging to the United States; and nothing in this Constitution shall be so construed as to Prejudice any Claims of the United States, or of any particular State.

*Changed by the Eleventh Amendment.
**Changed by the Thirteenth Amendment.

Section 4.

Republican Government Guaranteed

The United States shall guarantee to every State in this Union a Republican Form of Government, and shall protect each of them against Invasion; and on Application of the Legislature, or of the Executive (when the Legislature cannot be convened) against domestic Violence.

ARTICLE V.

Amendment Procedures

The Congress, whenever two thirds of both Houses shall deem it necessary, shall propose Amendments to this Constitution, or, on the Application of the Legislatures of two thirds of the several States, shall call a Convention for proposing Amendments, which, in either Case, shall be valid to all Intents and Purposes, as Part of this Constitution, when ratified by the Legislatures of three fourths of the several States, or by Conventions in three fourths thereof, as the one or the other Mode of Ratification may be proposed by the Congress; Provided that no Amendment which may be made prior to the Year One thousand eight hundred and eight shall in any Manner affect the first and fourth Clauses in the Ninth Section of the first Article; and that no State, without its Consent, shall be deprived of its equal Suffrage in the Senate.

ARTICLE VI.

Supremacy of the Constitution and Federal Laws

1. All debts contracted and Engagements entered into, before the Adoption of this Constitution, shall be as valid against the United States under this Constitution, as under the Confederation.

2. This Constitution, and the Laws of the United States which shall be made in Pursuance thereof; and all Treaties made, or which shall be made, under the Authority of the United States, shall be the supreme Law of the Land; and the Judges in every State shall be bound thereby, any Thing in the Constitution or Laws of any State to the Contrary notwithstanding.

3. The Senators and Representatives before mentioned, and the Members of the several State Legislatures, and all executive and judicial Officers, both of the United States and of the several States, shall be bound by Oath or Affirmation, to support this Constitution; but no religious Test shall ever be required as a Qualification to any Office or public Trust under the United States.

ARTICLE VII.

Ratification

The Ratification of the Conventions of nine States, shall be sufficient for the Establishment of this Constitution between the States so ratifying the Same.

Done in Convention by the unanimous consent of the States present the seventeenth day of September in the year of our Lord one thousand seven hundred and eighty seven and of the Independence of the United States of America the Twelfth. In witness whereof we have hereunto subscribed our Names,

George Washington — President
and deputy from Virginia

This constitution was adopted on September 17, 1787 by the Constitutional Convention, and was declared ratified on July 2, 1788.

Signers of the Constitution

New Hampshire

John Langdon

Nicholas Gilman

Massachusetts

Nathaniel Gorham

Rufus King

Connecticut

William Samuel Johnson

Roger Sherman

New York

Alexander Hamilton

New Jersey

William Livingston

David Brearley

William Paterson

Jonathan Dayton

Pennsylvania

Benjamin Franklin

Thomas Mifflin

Robert Morris

George Clymer

Thomas Fitzsimons

Jared Ingersoll

James Wilson

Gouverneur Morris

Delaware

George Read

Gunning Bedford, Jr.

John Dickinson

Richard Bassett

Jacob Broom

Maryland

James McHenry

Daniel of St. Tho. Jenifer

Daniel Carrol

Virginia

John Blair

James Madison, Junior

North Carolina

William Blount

Richard Dobbs Spaight

Hugh Williamson

South Carolina

John Rutledge

Charles Cotesworth Pinckney

Charles Pinckney

Pierce Butler

Georgia

William Few

Abraham Baldwin

Attest *William Jackson*
Secretary

Amendments to the Constitution

Since 1787, twenty-six amendments have been proposed by the Congress and ratified by the several states, pursuant to the fifth Article of the original Constitution.

Amendment I.

Freedom of Religion and Expression

Congress shall make no law respecting an establishment of religion, or prohibiting the free exercise thereof; or abridging the freedom of speech, or of the press, or the right of the people peaceably to assemble, and to petition the Government for a redress of grievances. (Ratified December, 1791.)

Amendment II.

Right to Bear Arms

A well regulated Militia, being necessary to the security of a free State, the right of the people to keep and bear Arms, shall not be infringed. (Ratified December, 1791.)

Amendment III.

Quartering of Soldiers

No Soldier shall, in time of peace be quartered in any house, without the consent of the Owner, nor in time of war, but in a manner to be prescribed by law. (Ratified December, 1791.)

Amendment IV.

Security From Unreasonable Searches and Seizures

The right of the people to be secure in their persons, houses, papers, and effects, against unreasonable searches and seizures, shall not be violated, and no Warrants shall issue, but upon probable cause, supported by Oath or affirmation, and particularly describing the place to be searched, and the persons or things to be seized. (Ratified December, 1791.)

Amendment V.

Rights of Due Process of Law

No person shall be held to answer for a capital, or otherwise infamous crime, unless on a presentment or indictment of a Grand Jury, except in cases arising in the land or naval forces, or in the Militia, when in actual service in time of War or public danger; nor shall any person be subject for the same offence to be twice put in jeopardy of life or limb, nor shall be compelled in any criminal case to be a witness against himself, nor be deprived of life, liberty, or property, without due process of law; nor shall private property be taken for public use without just compensation. (Ratified December, 1791.)

Amendment VI.

Right to a Fair Trial

In all criminal prosecutions, the accused shall enjoy the right to a speedy and public trial, by an impartial jury of the State and district wherein the crime shall have been committed; which district shall have been previously ascertained by law, and to be informed of the nature and cause of the accusation; to be confronted with the witnesses against him; to have compulsory process for obtaining witnesses in his favor, and to have the assistance of counsel for his defence. (Ratified December, 1791.)

Amendment VII.

Trial by Jury

In Suits at common law, where the value in controversy shall exceed twenty dollars, the right of trial by jury shall be preserved, and no fact tried by a jury shall be otherwise re-examined in any Court of the United States, than according to the rules of the common law. (Ratified December, 1791.)

Amendment VIII.

Fair Bail and Punishments

Excessive bail shall not be required, nor excessive fines imposed, nor cruel and unusual punishments inflicted. (Ratified December, 1791.)

Amendment IX.

Rights Retained by the People

The enumeration in the Constitution of certain rights shall not be construed to deny or disparage others retained by the people. (Ratified December, 1791.)

Amendment X.

Powers Reserved to States and People

The powers not delegated to the United States by the Constitution, nor prohibited by it to the States, are reserved to the States respectively, or to the people. (Ratified December, 1791.)

Amendment XI.

Limitations on Federal Courts

The Judicial power of the United States shall not be construed to extend to any suit in law or equity, commenced or prosecuted against one of the United States by Citizens of another State, or by Citizens or Subjects of any Foreign State. (Ratified February, 1795.)

Amendment XII.

Election of President

The Electors shall meet in their respective states, and vote by ballot for President and Vice President, one of whom, at least, shall not be an inhabitant of the same state with themselves; they shall name in their ballots the person voted for as President, and in distinct ballots the person voted for as Vice-President, and they shall make distinct lists of all persons voted for as President, and of all persons voted for as Vice-President, and of the number of votes for each, which lists they shall sign and certify, and transmit sealed to the seat of the government of the United States, directed to the President of the Senate;—The President of the Senate shall, in the presence of the Senate and House of Representatives, open all the certificates and the votes shall then be counted;—The person having the greatest number of votes for President, shall be the President, if such number be a majority of the whole number of Electors appointed; and if no person have such majority, then from the persons having the highest numbers not exceeding three on the list of those voted for as President, the House of Representatives shall choose immediately, by ballot, the President. But in choosing the President, the votes shall be taken by states, the representation from each state having one vote; a quorum for this purpose shall consist of a member or members from two-thirds of the states, and a majority of all the states shall be necessary to a choice. [And if the House of Representatives shall not choose a President whenever the right of choice shall devolve upon them, before the fourth day of March next following, then the Vice-President shall act as President, as in the case of the death or other constitutional disability of the President—]* The person having the greatest number of votes as Vice-President, shall be the Vice-President, if such number be a majority of the whole number of Electors appointed, and if no person have a majority, then from the two highest numbers on the list, the Senate shall choose the Vice-President; a quorum for the purpose shall consist of two-thirds of the whole number of Senators, and a majority of the whole number shall be necessary to a choice. But no person constitutionally ineligible to the office of President shall be eligible to that of Vice-President of the United States. (Ratified June, 1804.)

Amendment XIII.

Slavery Abolished

Section 1. Neither slavery nor involuntary servitude, except as a punishment for crime whereof the party shall have been duly convicted, shall exist within the United States, or any place subject to their jurisdiction.

Section 2. Congress shall have power to enforce this article by appropriate legislation. (Ratified December, 1865.)

Amendment XIV.

Equal Protection and Due Process; Citizenship Defined and Guaranteed

Section 1. All persons born or naturalized in the United States and subject to the jurisdiction thereof, are citizens of the United States and of the State wherein they reside. No State shall make or enforce any law which shall abridge the privileges or immunities of citizens of the United States; nor shall any State deprive any person of life, liberty, or property, without due process of law; nor deny to any person within its jurisdiction the equal protection of the laws.

Section 2. Representatives shall be apportioned among the several States according to their respective numbers, counting the whole number of persons in each State, excluding Indians not taxed. But when the right to vote at any election for the choice of electors for President and Vice President of the United States, Representatives in Congress, the Executive and Judicial officers of a State, or the members of the Legislature thereof, is denied to any of the male inhabitants of such State, being twenty-one years of age, and citizens of the United States, or in any way abridged, except for participation in rebellion, or other crime, the basis of representation therein shall be reduced in the proportion

*Superseded by section 3 of the Twentieth Amendment.

which the number of such male citizens shall bear to the whole number of male citizens twenty-one years of age in such State.

Section 3. No person shall be a Senator or a Representative in Congress, or elector of President and Vice President, or hold any office, civil or military, under the United States, or under any State, who, having previously taken an oath, as a member of Congress, or as an officer of the United States, or as a member of any State legislature, or as an executive or judicial officer of any State, to support the Constitution of the United States, shall have engaged in insurrection or rebellion against the same, or given aid or comfort to the enemies thereof. But Congress may by a vote of two-thirds of each House, remove such disability.

Section 4. The validity of the public debt of the United States, authorized by law, including debts incurred for payment of pensions and bounties for services in suppressing insurrection or rebellion, shall not be questioned. But neither the United States nor any State shall assume or pay any debt or obligation incurred in aid of insurrection or rebellion against the United States, or any claim for the loss or emancipation of any slave; but all such debts, obligations and claims shall be held illegal and void.

Section 5. The Congress shall have power to enforce, by appropriate legislation, the provisions of this article. (Ratified July, 1868.)

Amendment XV.

Blacks' Right to Vote

Section 1. The right of citizens of the United States to vote shall not be denied or abridged by the United States or by any State on account of race, color, or previous condition of servitude.

Section 2. The Congress shall have power to enforce this article by appropriate legislation. (Ratified February, 1870.)

Amendment XVI.

Power to Tax Incomes

The Congress shall have power to lay and collect taxes on incomes, from whatever source derived, without apportionment among the several States, and without regard to any census or enumeration. (Ratified February, 1913.)

Amendment XVII.

Popular Election of Senators

The Senate of the United States shall be composed of two Senators from each State, elected by the people thereof, for six years; and each Senator shall have one vote. The electors in each State shall have the qualifications requisite for electors of the most numerous branch of the State legislatures.

When vacancies happen in the representation of any State in the Senate, the executive authority of such State shall issue writs of election to fill such vacancies: Provided, That the legislature of any State may empower the executive thereof to make temporary appointments until the people fill the vacancies by election as the legislature may direct.

This amendment shall not be so construed as to affect the election or term of any Senator chosen before it becomes valid as part of the Constitution. (Ratified April, 1913.)

Amendment XVIII.

Prohibition of Alcoholic Beverages

[Section 1. After one year from the ratification of this article the manufacture, sale, or transportation of intoxicating liquors within, the importation thereof into, or the exportation thereof from the United States and all territory subject to the jurisdiction thereof for beverage purposes is hereby prohibited.

Section 2. The Congress and the several States shall have concurrent power to enforce this article by appropriate legislation.

Section 3. This article shall be inoperative unless it shall have been ratified as an amendment to the Constitution by the legislatures of the several States, as provided in the Constitution, within seven years from the date of the submission hereof to the States by the Congress.]* (Ratified January, 1919.)

Amendment XIX.

Female Suffrage

The right of citizens of the United States to vote shall not be denied or abridged by the United States or by any State on account of sex.

Congress shall have power to enforce this article by appropriate legislation. (Ratified August, 1920.)

*Repealed by the Twenty-First Amendment.

Amendment XX.
Changes in Terms of President and Congress

Section 1. The terms of the President and Vice President shall end at noon on the 20th day of January, and the terms of Senators and Representatives at noon on the 3d day of January, of the years in which such terms would have ended if this article had not been ratified; and the terms of their successors shall then begin.

Section 2. The Congress shall assemble at least once in every year, and such meeting shall begin at noon on the 3d day of January, unless they shall by law appoint a different day.

Section 3. If, at the time fixed for the beginning of the term of the President, the President elect shall have died, the Vice President elect shall become President. If a President shall not have been chosen before the time fixed for the beginning of his term, or if the President elect shall have failed to qualify, then the Vice President elect shall act as President until a President shall have qualified; and the Congress may by law provide for the case wherein neither a President elect nor a Vice President elect shall have qualified, declaring who shall then act as President, or the manner in which one who is to act shall be selected, and such person shall act accordingly until a President or Vice President shall have qualified.

Section 4. The Congress may by law provide for the case of the death of any of the persons from whom the House of Representatives may choose a President whenever the right of choice shall have devolved upon them, and for the case of the death of any of the persons from whom the Senate may choose a Vice President whenever the right of choice shall have devolved upon them.

Section 5. Sections 1 and 2 shall take effect on the 15th day of October following the ratification of this article.

Section 6. This article shall be inoperative unless it shall have been ratified as an amendment to the Constitution by the legislatures of three-fourths of the several States within seven years from the date of its submission. (Ratified January, 1933.)

Amendment XXI.
Repeal of Alcohol Prohibition

Section 1. The eighteenth article of amendment to the Constitution of the United States is hereby repealed.

Section 2. The transportation or importation into any State, Territory, or possession of the United States for delivery or use therein of intoxicating liquors, in violation of the laws thereof, is hereby prohibited.

Section 3. This article shall be inoperative unless it shall have been ratified as an amendment to the Constitution by conventions in the several States, as provided in the Constitution, within seven years from the date of the submission hereof to the States by the Congress. (Ratified December, 1933.)

Amendment XXII.
President Limited to Two Terms

Section 1. No person shall be elected to the office of the President more than twice, and no person who has held the office of President, or acted as President, for more than two years of a term to which some other person was elected President shall be elected to the office of the President more than once. But this Article shall not apply to any person holding the office of President when this Article was proposed by the Congress, and shall not prevent any person who may be holding the office of President, or acting as President, during the term within which this Article becomes operative from holding the office of President or acting as President during the remainder of such term.

Section 2. This article shall be inoperative unless it shall have been ratified as an amendment to the Constitution by the legislatures of three-fourths of the several States within seven years from the date of its submission to the States by the Congress. (Ratified February, 1951.)

Amendment XXIII.
Presidential Suffrage for District of Columbia

Section 1. The District constituting the seat of Government of the United States shall appoint in such manner as the Congress may direct:

A number of electors of President and Vice President equal to the whole number of Senators and Representatives in Congress to which the District would be entitled if it were a State, but in no event more than the least populous State; they shall be in addition to those appointed by the States, but they shall be considered, for the purposes of the election of President and Vice President, to be electors appointed by a State; and they shall meet in the District and perform such duties as provided by the twelfth article of amendment.

Section 2. The Congress shall have power to enforce this article by appropriate legislation. (Ratified March, 1961.)

Amendment XXIV.

Poll Tax Forbidden

Section 1. The right of citizens of the United States to vote in any primary or other election for President or Vice President, for electors for President or Vice President, or for Senator or Representative in Congress, shall not be denied or abridged by the United States or any State by reason of failure to pay any poll tax or other tax.

Section 2. The Congress shall have power to enforce this article by appropriate legislation. (Ratified January, 1964.)

Amendment XXV.

Procedures for Presidential Succession

Section 1. In case of the removal of the President from office or of his death or resignation, the Vice President shall become President.

Section 2. Whenever there is a vacancy in the office of the Vice President, the President shall nominate a Vice President who shall take office upon confirmation by a majority vote of both Houses of Congress.

Section 3. Whenever the President transmits to the President pro tempore of the Senate and the Speaker of the House of Representatives his written declaration that he is unable to discharge the powers and duties of his office, and until he transmits to them a written declaration to the contrary, such powers and duties shall be discharged by the Vice President as Acting President.

Section 4. Whenever the Vice President and a majority of either the principal officers of the executive departments or of such other body as Congress may by law provide, transmit to the President pro tempore of the Senate and the Speaker of the House of Representatives their written declaration that the President is unable to discharge the powers and duties of his office, the Vice President shall im-

mediately assume the powers and duties of the office as Acting President.

Thereafter, when the President transmits to the President pro tempore of the Senate and the Speaker of the House of Representatives his written declaration that no inability exists, he shall resume the powers and duties of his office unless the Vice President and a majority of either the principal officers of the executive department or of such other body as Congress may by law provide, transmit within four days to the President pro tempore of the Senate and the Speaker of the House of Representatives their written declaration that the President is unable to discharge the powers and duties of his office. Thereupon Congress shall decide the issue, assembling within forty-eight hours for that purpose if not in session. If the Congress, within twenty-one days after receipt of the latter written declaration, or, if Congress is not in session, within twenty-one days after Congress is required to assemble, determines by two-thirds vote of both Houses that the President is unable to discharge the powers and duties of his office, the Vice President shall continue to discharge the same as Acting President; otherwise, the President shall resume the powers and duties of his office. (Ratified February, 1967.)

Amendment XXVI.

Voting Age Lowered to Eighteen

Section 1. The right of citizens of the United States, who are eighteen years of age or older, to vote shall not be denied or abridged by the United States or by any State on account of age.

Section 2. The Congress shall have power to enforce this article by appropriate legislation. (Ratified July, 1971.)

Amendment XXVII

No law varying the compensation for the services of the Senators or Representatives, shall take effect, until an election of Representatives shall have intervened. (Ratified May, 1992.)

This is the original text and section numbers. Descriptive headings have been added by editors. Passages in brackets indicate that they were changed by Amendments.

Bibliography

General

Cooke, Edward F. *A Detailed Analysis of the Constitution.* Totowa, NJ: Rowman & Allenheld, 1984.

Kelly, Alfred H., and Winfred A. Harbison. *The American Constitution: Its Origins and Development.* New York: W. W. Norton, 1983.

Kurland, Philip B., and Ralph Lerner. *The Founders' Constitution.* 5 vols. Chicago and London: The University of Chicago Press, 1987.

Levy, Leonard, Kenneth L. Karst, and Dennis Mahoney, eds. *Encyclopedia of the American Constitution.* 4 vols. New York: MacMillan Publishing Company, 1986.

Mitchell, Ralph, ed. *C Q's Guide to the United States Constitution.* Washington, D.C.: Congressional Quarterly, 1986.

Peltason, J. W. *Corwin and Peltason's Understanding the Constitution.* New York: Holt, Rinehart, & Winston, 1982.

Pritchett, C. Herman. *The American Constitution.* New York: McGraw-Hill Book Company, Inc., 1959, 3rd ed., 1977.

Smith, Page. *The Constitution: A Documentary and Narrative History.* New York: Morrow, Quill, 1980.

Unit One: What is government?

1. Primary Sources.

Locke, John. *Two Treatises of Government.* ed. Peter Laslett. New York: Mentor Books, New American Library, 1965. (Other editions are also available)

Hamilton, Alexander, James Madison, and John Jay. *The Federalist.* ed. Jacob E. Cooke. Middletown, Conn.: Wesleyan University Press, 1961.

Montesquieu, Baron de. *The Spirit of the Laws.* (1748) Trans. Thomas Nugent.

2. Secondary Sources.

Corwin, Edward S. *The "Higher Law" Background of American Constitutional Law.* Ithaca: Cornell University Press, 1955.

McIlwain, Charles H. *Constitutionalism, Ancient and Modern.* Ithaca: Great Seal Books, 1958.

Sabine, George. *A History of Political Theory.* New York: Holt, Rinehart, & Winston, 1965.

Unit Two: What experiences shaped the Founders' thinking about government?

1. Primary sources.

The Founders' Constitution, op. cit., vol.1. "Fundamental Documents," pp. 1-28; "Popular Basis of Political Authority," pp. 39-74; "Right to Revolution," pp. 77-95; "Deficiencies of the Confederation," pp. 147-183.

Morison, Samuel Eliot, ed. *Sources and Documents Illustrating the American Revolution, 1764-1788 and the Foundation of the Federal Constitution.* 2nd edition, 1929. Reprint. Oxford: The Clarendon Press, 1948.

Smith, James M., and Paul Murphy. *Liberty and Justice: A Historical Record of American Constitutional Development,* 1968.

2. Secondary sources.

Bailyn, Bernard. *The Ideological Origins of the American Revolution.* Cambridge: Harvard University Press, 1967.

Becker, Carl. *The Declaration of Independence: A Study in the History of Ideas.* New York: Alfred A. Knopf, Inc., 1966.

Kammen, Michael. *Deputies and Liberties: The Origins of Representative Government in America.* 1972.

Jensen, Merrill. *The New Nation.* Boston: Northeastern University Press, 1981.

Middlekauff, Robert. *The Glorious Cause: The American Revolution, 1763-1789.* New York: Oxford University Press, 1982.

Wills, Garry. *Inventing America: Jefferson's Declaration of Independence.* Garden City: Doubleday, 1978.

Wood, Gordon. *The Creation of the American Republic.* New York: W.W. Norton, 1972.

Unit Three: What happened at the Philadelphia Convention?

1. Primary Sources:

The Founders' Constitution, op. cit., vols. 3-4, passim; vol. 2, "Convention," pp. 185-205.

Kammen, Michael, ed. *The Origins of the American Constitution: A Documentary History.* New York: Penguin Books, 1986.

Lewis, John D., ed. *Anti-Federalists versus Federalists: Selected Documents.* San Francisco: Chandler Publishing Company, 1967.

Madison, James. *The Records of the Federal Convention of 1787,* ed. Max Farrand. 4 vols. New Haven and London: Yale University Press, 1966.

Pole, J. R., ed. *The American Constitution, For and Against: The Federalist and Anti-Federalist Papers.* New York: Hill and Wang, 1987.

Storing, Herbert. *The Complete Anti-Federalist.* 7 vols. Chicago: University of Chicago Press, 1981.

2. Secondary sources.

Berns, Walter. *The Writing of the United States Constitution.* Washington, D.C.: American Enterprise Institute, 1985.

Bernstein, Richard. *Are We to be a Nation? The Making of the Constitution.* Cambridge: Harvard University Press, 1987.

Bowen, Catherine Drinker. *Miracle at Philadelphia.* Boston & Toronto: Little, Brown, & Co., 1986.

Collier, James L. and Christopher Collier. *Decision in Philadelphia.* New York: Random House, 1985.

Farrand, Max. *The Framing of the Constitution of the United States.* 1913. Reprint. New Haven and London: Yale University Press, 1987.

Levy, Leonard W., ed. *Essays on the Making of the Constitution.* 1987. Reprint. New York: Oxford University Press, 1987.

McDonald, Forrest. *E Pluribus Unum: The Formation of the American Republic, 1776-1790.* Indianapolis: Liberty Press, 1979.

Morris, Richard B. *Witnesses at the Creation: Hamilton, Madison, Jay, and the Constitution.* New York: Holt, Rinehart, & Winston, 1985.

Rodell, Fred. *55 Men: The Story of the Constitution.* New York: Macmillan Publishing Company, 1966.

Rutland, Robert A. *The Ordeal of the Constitution: The Anti-Federalists and the Ratification Struggle of 1787-88.* Norman: University of Oklahoma Press, 1966.

Van Doren, Carl. *The Great Rehearsal.* Westport, Conn.: Greenwood Press, 1982.

Unit Four: How was the Constitution used to establish our government?

1. Primary Sources

Founders' Constitution, op. cit., vol. 5, "Bill of Rights," pp. 1-42; "Article 3, Section 1" (Judicial system), vol. 5, pp. 131-211.

2. Secondary Sources

Hall, Kermit L. *The Supreme Court and Judicial Review in American History.* (Bicentennial Essays on the Constitution). Washington, D.C.: American Historical Association, 1985.

Levy, Leonard B. *Judicial Review and the Supreme Court.* New York: Harper & Row, 1967.

McCloskey, Robert. *The American Supreme Court.* Chicago: University of Chicago Press, 1960.

McCloskey, Robert. *The Modern Supreme Court.* Cambridge: Harvard University Press, 1972.

Nowak, John. *Constitutional Law.* St. Paul: West Publishing Company, 1983.

Roche, John Pearson, and Leonard Levy. *The Judiciary.* New York: Harcourt, Brace, & World, 1964.

Rutland, Robert A. *The Birth of the Bill of Rights: Its Origin and Meaning.* Indianapolis: Liberty Press, 1965.

Unit Five: How does the Constitution protect our basic rights?

1. Primary sources

Founders' Constitution, vol. 5, (Amendments I-X), pp. 43-473.

2. Secondary Sources

American Academy of Political and Social Sciences. *The Revolution, The Constitution, and America's Third Century: The Bicentennial Conference on the U. S. Constitution.* Philadelphia: University of Pennsylvania Press, 1981.

Berns, Walter. *The First Amendment and the Future of American Democracy.* New York: Basic Books, 1976.

Cortner, Richard C. *The Supreme Court and the Second Bill of Rights.* Madison: University of Wisconsin Press, 1981.

Cox, Archibald. *The Role of the Supreme Court in American Government.* Oxford: Oxford University Press, 1976.

Goldwin, Robert A., and William A. Schambra. *How Does the Constitution Secure Rights?* 1984.

Hand, Learned. *The Bill of Rights.* Cambridge: Harvard University Press, 1958.

Morgan, David. *Suffragists and Democrats: The Politics of Women Suffrage in America.* East Lansing: Michigan State University Press, 1972.

Murphy, Paul L. *The Constitution in the Twentieth Century.* (Bicentennial Essays on the Constitution). Washington, D.C.: American Historical Association, 1986.

Unit Six: What are the responsibilities of citizens?

1. Primary Sources

Aristotle, *Politics,* ed. Ernest Barker. 1958. Reprint. New York: Oxford University Press, 1968. Bk. III, Chs. 1-5.

Founders' Constitution, vol.2, "Citizenship," pp. 557-619.

Rousseau, Jean-Jacques. *The Social Contract.*

2. Secondary Sources.

Tussman, Joseph. *Obligation and the Body Politic.* New York: Oxford University Press, 1960.

Walzer, Michael. *Obligations: Essays on Disobedience, War and Citizenship.* Cambridge: Harvard University Press, 1970.

Note: Many of these books are available in paperback editions.

Reference Material for a Federalist
Anti-Federalist Debate

Federalists' Position

The following information summarizes the arguments presented for the Federalists' position in the series of essays which are entitled *The Federalist*. These essays were by Alexander Hamilton, John Jay, and James Madison. They used a common pen-name, Publius, a patriot of ancient Rome.

I. Republican Government

Most people had thought that republican government could only exist in a small territory populated by people who possessed civic virtue. Publius argued that republican government is the only form of government suited to the spirit of Americans. He also maintained that it is possible to have republican government in a territory as large as that represented by the thirteen original states. Moreover, he maintained that it is possible to have republican government even if the people lack civic virtue. His most controversial claim was that such a republic, an extended republic, as he called it, would be superior to the classical republics of small city-states which depended on the civic virtue of the citizens.

In *Federalist* #10, he described what he thought was the major problem of the classical republics. That problem was what he called "faction." When he spoke of factions, he was referring to what we now call interest groups. These factions are made up of people of common interests or beliefs who try to get the government to do things that are desirable for them but which are contrary to the common good.

The old doctrines of republicanism had held that the main way of preventing this kind of behavior was for the citizens to possess civic virtue. That is, virtuous citizens would prefer the common good to their own particular interests. The encouragement of this kind of behavior would be accomplished by education, religion, and the good example of those who exercised political authority. Publius argued, however, that history demonstrated that this does not work. The old republics had been destroyed because people preferred their own interests to the good of the community.

A larger state could avoid these problems, Publius thought. This was so because the people would be dispersed over a large territory. A larger number of people would produce a greater number of interest groups. These interest groups, scattered over a large territory, would find it impossible to cooperate with one another in order to form majorities, get the government to do what they wanted, and obtain laws that were favorable to their own interests instead of the common interest. In addition, representation and checks and balances would also help to ensure that the common interest rather than private interests would influence the policy of the government. Thus, the extended republic solved one of the most important problems of the old republics and clearly represented a superior form of republican government.

II. Federalism

The Constitution established a new kind of political system: a federal system. In such a system, there are two governments, each sovereign in its own sphere and each with the authority to act directly upon the people. Previously there had been confederations which were collections of sovereign states. (The United Nations might be thought of as a sort of confederation.) Most frequently these confederations consisted of a group of sovereign states held together by treaties for mutual defense or for purposes of trade. The other form of government had been national or consolidated, in which all authority had been located in one central government.

The United States under the Articles of Confederation had been, as the name suggests, a confederation. The central government, such as it was, had very little authority. It could not, for example, tax the people directly. It could only request money from the states, and if the states did not pay the amounts requested, there was not anything the government (Congress) could do. Moreover, it could not pass any laws directly affecting the people, which made it difficult to enter into treaties with foreign countries or even to regulate trade among the states.

Publius argued that this had made the United States weak and disreputable abroad and disunited at home. He insisted that in order to solve these problems, there was a need for a national government with the authority to deal with those problems common to all of the states. These included foreign affairs, i.e., treaty and war-making powers. There is a clear need, he also argued, for a common authority to regulate commerce, coin money, and enforce contracts in order to restore the economy of the United States. All of this was necessary, he said, if the government was to be able to provide for the general defense and security as well as the common welfare of the United States.

This, he went out of his way to say, did not mean that the state governments were to be eliminated or made entirely subordinate to the government of the United States in regard to matters of purely local jurisdiction. It is true that under the Constitution, the laws passed by Congress are the supreme law of the land, but only in those matters over which Congress is given authority by the Constitution, and these are the powers enumerated in Article I, section 8 of the Constitution.

These powers should not be feared, Publius argued, because in any contest between the states and the national government, the advantage is on the side of the state governments. The state governments, being closer to the people than the national government, will have a greater claim to their loyalty and support. In fact, he argued, the greatest problem under the new Constitution will not come from the power of the national government but from the powers retained by the states. This is so in spite of the supremacy clause of the Constitution.

III. Separation of powers and checks and balances

Virtually all Americans in 1787 agreed that the separation of powers is the keystone of constitutional (limited) government. In *Federalist #47*, Publius wrote, "The accumulation of all powers, legislative, executive, and judiciary, in the same hands, whether of one, a few, or many, and whether hereditary, self-appointed, or elective, may justly be pronounced the very definition of tyranny."

However, critics of the Constitution pointed out that while the legislative, executive, and judicial powers were indeed placed in three separate branches, these powers were not completely distinct. Through the veto, the executive was involved in the legislative power. Through the authority to approve appointments and treaties, the legislative branch was involved in the executive power. These were merely two examples mentioned as violations of the principle of separation of powers.

Publius argued that if the three branches of government were totally separate, it would be impossible for them to check and balance each other. Hence, they must be armed with the power to do so. The new Constitution gives them this power. The executive can check the legislative branch through the use of the veto power. The legislative branch can check the executive by over-riding the veto by a two-thirds vote in the House and Senate. These and other devices provided by the Constitution ensure that the three branches of government will be kept in balance.

IV. The House of Representatives

Major objections were voiced by opponents to the two-year term and the relatively small number of representatives. Many believed that annual elections were required to keep the representatives responsible to their constituents. They also argued that one representative for 30,000 people was insufficient to provide for representative government.

Publius argued that elections every two years are sufficient to protect the safety of the people. He also maintained that two-year terms are desirable because they would enable the representatives to get more experience without making them so independent of the people's judgment as to become dangerous.

In answer to the claim that there are too few representatives, Publius argued that the limited power given to Congress makes it safe to entrust the legislative authority of the lower house to a fairly small number of persons. In addition, he appealed to the "vigilant and manly" spirit of Americans. "I am unable to conceive that the people of America, in their present temper, or under any circumstances which can speedily happen, will choose, and every year repeat the choice of sixty-five or a hundred men who would be disposed to form and pursue a scheme of tyranny or treachery."

Finally, he defended the number of representatives by arguing that the larger the assembly, the smaller the number of people who actually direct its affairs. This is so because large groups are more susceptible to the appeal of emotion and are more likely to be swayed by the appeals of clever and unscrupulous demagogues.

V. The Senate

Publius addressed four objections that had been raised regarding the Senate.

1. The qualifications for senators were more advanced age and a longer period of citizenship. (Senators were required to be at least 30 years of age and citizens for 9 years preceding election. Members of the House of Representatives must be 25 years old and citizens for 7 years.) He argued that the office of senator requires greater knowledge and stability of character. Since senators deal with foreign nations through the treaty-making power, they should be free of foreign influences, and this is more likely if they have been citizens for a longer period of time.

2. In response to objections over the appointment of senators by state legislatures, he claimed that this was the method favored by public opinion and also is useful as a means of linking the state governments to the federal government.

3. He defended the equal representation of each state in the Senate by candidly admitting that this was a compromise between the claims of the large states and the small states. He went on to claim that it is desirable for laws to require approval by a majority of the people and a majority of the states. He admitted that this might seem an inconvenience, making it more difficult to pass laws. But this may be a good thing because "the facility and excess of law-making seem to be the diseases to which our governments are most liable . . . ."

4. To those who were suspicious of the small number of senators, Madison insisted that it would result in greater stability and dignity in the government. He argued that large assemblies are susceptible to sudden and violent passions. A small body, elected for six-year terms, would be more sober and better informed in its deliberations. The resulting stability would be advantageous both in terms of domestic politics and foreign relations.

VI. The President

Publius had harsh words for critics of the presidency, who have "decorated" this office with "attributes superior in dignity and splendor to those of a King of Great Britain." He first addressed the selection of the president by the electoral college, a group of men chosen specifically for the purpose. This method, he claimed, would remove the selection of the president from tumult and disorder. Meeting in their several states, members of the electoral college would be less susceptible to intrigues and conspiracies. Describing the process by which the selection of the president might be made by the House of Representatives, he concluded, "This process of election affords a moral certainty that the office of president will seldom fall to the lot of any man who is not in an eminent degree endowed with the requisite qualifications." The result will be "a constant probability of seeing the station filled by characters pre-eminent for ability and virtue."

To those who argued that a strong executive is incompatible with republican government, Publius retorted that energy in the executive is the first prerequisite of good government. "It is essential to the protection of the community against foreign attacks; it is not less essential to the steady administration of the laws; to the protection of property against those irregular and high-handed combinations which sometimes interrupt the ordinary course of justice; to the security of liberty against the enterprises and assaults of ambition, of faction, and anarchy." He cited the example of Rome to demonstrate that a strong executive branch is essential for preventing the people from taking "refuge in the absolute power of a single man, under the formidable title of dictator . . ." A feeble executive, he insisted, leads to weak government and such a government, "whatever it may be in theory, must be, in practice, a bad government."

There were some people who argued in favor of a plural executive. Publius held that a plural executive is deficient in performing the executive functions, necessarily lacking secrecy, dispatch, and decisiveness. Moreover, a plural executive tends to conceal faults and destroy responsibility. Finally, he pointed out, a plural executive is more expensive than a single executive.

Defending the four-year term, Publius claimed that it would give the executive a certain independence from the transient whim and passing opinions of the people, which is desirable. "The republican principle demands that the deliberate sense of the community should govern the conduct of those to whom they entrust the management of their affairs; but it does not require an unqualified compliance to every sudden breeze of passion, or to every transient impulse which the people may receive from the acts of men, who flatter their prejudices to betray their interests." The people always intend the public good, but sometimes they are led astray. A statesman, he agreed, and especially the executive, should be able to resist these momentary impulses and act on the basis of long-term calculations of the public good, unswayed by the passion of the moment.

He defended re-eligibility for election on similar grounds. He also argued that it lends stability to the government, providing a degree of continuity in its administration which is advantageous from the point of view of both domestic and foreign policy.

Having defended the great powers of the executive, Publius asked if it is safe to entrust the people's liberties to a government with such an executive. The people of the United States, given their experience with the British monarch and the royal governors, were naturally suspicious of executive power. Publius assured them that the executive power established by the Constitution is not only effective, but it is also safe. He gave two reasons. The president is chosen every four years by persons (electoral college) "immediately chosen by the people for that purpose," and he is liable to impeachment, trial, and dismissal from office. Moreover, effective controls upon the executive power are provided by the system of checks and balances, in which some of the most important powers (treaty-making and appointive) are shared with the Senate. These measures, agreed Publius, provide assurance that executive power would not be successfully abused.

VII. The Judiciary

Questions were raised by opponents of the Constitution regarding the way in which judges were appointed and their lifetime tenure in office during good behavior.

Publius dismissed the first by pointing out that while judges are appointed by the president, his appointments require the advice and consent of the Senate. This, he suggested, is sufficient to guard against foolish appointments.

Life tenure he defended by first arguing that the judicial power, having access to neither the sword nor the purse, is the least dangerous branch of the government. "The Judiciary is beyond comparison the weakest of the three departments of power . . . ."

Having argued that it is safe to entrust the judicial power to judges with life tenure, he also said it is necessary in order to guarantee their independence. The independence of the judiciary is especially important under a Constitution providing for a government of limited powers. Such a Constitution stipulates that there are certain kinds of laws, for example, ex post facto laws, that the legislature cannot pass. "Limitations of this kind," wrote Publius, "can be preserved in practice no other way than through the medium of courts of justice, whose duty it must be to declare all acts contrary to the manifest terms of the Constitution void. Without this, all the reservations of particular rights or privileges would amount to nothing."

Life tenure, Publius emphasized, is essential if the judges are to possess the independence necessary for performing the "arduous" task of enforcing the limits imposed by the Constitution on the other branches of government. Moreover, the duties of judges require great amounts of knowledge and experience which would be enhanced by lengthy terms of service.

VIII. Bill of Rights

Publius responded to complaints that the Constitution does not contain a bill of rights. After pointing out that some of the state constitutions do not have a bill of rights, he argued that the Constitution contains protection for those rights usually mentioned in bills of rights. These included the guarantee of habeas corpus, the prohibition of ex post facto laws, the guarantee in criminal cases of trial by jury in the state where the crime was committed, protection of persons and their descendants accused of treason, and the prohibition of titles of nobility. The latter he called "the cornerstone of republican government; for so long as they are excluded there can never be serious danger that the government will be any other than that of the people."

Most bills of rights, such as the Magna Carta, were between kings and their people, and are unnecessary in a political system where sovereignty resides in the people and the members of the government are only the people's servants. Moreover, a Constitution which delegates only limited powers to the government does not require a minutely detailed list of the rights maintained by the people.

Finally, Publius suggested that such a list of protected rights is in fact dangerous to the rights of the people. Why, he asked, provide protection against powers not granted? This, he suggested, might afford the pretext for the government to claim power it doesn't have on the ground that if protection is offered against the misuse of a particular power, that power must have been granted.

Publius concluded his defense of the Constitution with the following plea: "A Nation, without a National Government, is, in my view, an awful spectacle. The establishment of a Constitution, in time of profound peace, by the voluntary consent of a whole people, is a prodigy, to the completion of which I look forward with trembling anxiety."

The Anti-Federalists' Position

Unlike the Federalist, the Anti-Federalist position was not set forth in a single group of essays. Many speeches and pamphlets by a large number of opponents to the Constitution contain the various objections that were made.

I. Republican Government

The Anti-Federalists agreed that republican government was the only form of government suited to the United States. They, however, insisted that it was impossible to create and maintain a republican government in a territory as large and containing as many people as the thirteen states. One opponent wrote, "The idea of a . . . republic on an average one thousand miles in length and eight hundred in breadth, and containing six millions of white inhabitants . . . is in itself an absurdity, and contrary to the whole experience of mankind." It was true that a large republic was contrary to the experience of mankind as well as the teachings of writers such as Montesquieu. In arguing for "an extended republic," the Federalists had thought it possible to go beyond this experience and these teachings. The Anti-Federalists, on this as on other issues, were much more impressed with the lessons of the past. In this sense, at least, they were the conservatives in this debate.

Republicanism was the same as free or self-government. Such a government clearly requires the active support of the people. The Anti-Federalists argued that the government provided by the Constitution was too distant from the people to gain this support. The alternative was too horrible to contemplate, and was described by one opponent in the following words: "Nothing would support the government . . . but military coercion." And a writer in *The Independent Gazeteer* of Philadelphia warned, "From the moment we became one great Republic . . . the period is very shortly removed, when we shall sink finally into monarchy, and then into despotism."

Most of the writers on republicanism had assumed that it was possible only when the people had roughly the same economic status, pursued similar economic activities, lived their lives in similar ways, and had the same religious and moral points of view. The Anti-Federalists, who agreed, argued that this clearly was not the case in the United States. A New Englander observed, "The inhabitants of warmer climes are more dissolute in their manners, and less industrious, than in colder countries. . . . It is impossible for a code of laws to suit Georgia and Massachusetts." And a Southerner expressed a similar view when he wrote, "We see plainly that men who come from New England are different from us." He made it clear that he did not wish to be governed by or to govern with these different men.

Finally, many of the Anti-Federalists continued to insist that republican government required citizens who were virtuous. Writing under the name "Centinel," one argued that a government of checks and balances could not attain the common good. In a republic, he insisted, the people are sovereign and for the sovereign people to make good decisions, they must be virtuous. Moreover, they must be relatively equal, and that was less likely in a large nation than a small state.

II. Federalism

The Anti-Federalists were almost unanimous in their opposition to a "national" or "consolidated" government, and that, they insisted, was precisely the kind of government established by the Constitution. *The Federalist,* of course, denied this, arguing that the new federal government was a limited government of delegated powers, with the states retaining sovereignty over local matters. The Anti-Federalists were unimpressed with this argument. They based their opposition on four provisions of the Constitution: (1) the taxing power, (2) the provision for maintaining a standing army, (3) the necessary and proper clause, and (4) the supremacy clause.

Article I, Section 8 of the Constitution gave the federal government the power to levy taxes. This was a power Congress had not possessed under the Articles of Confederation and was viewed by the Framers as one of the major flaws of the Articles. In the minds of the Anti-Federalists, this provision alone made the new government a "consolidated" government. There was no doubt that such a government would become a tyrannical government. To give the government the power of the purse was to make it dangerously independent of the people. Worse, they believed the power to tax was the power to destroy, and conjured up horrible images of the people being bled dry by the overwhelming government. And the taxing power of the federal government may, it was claimed, be used to destroy the state governments. In Pennsylvania, one person warned,". . .the Congress may monopolize every source of revenue, and thus indirectly demolish the state government, for without funds they could not exist."

At least as bad as the taxing power, in the opponents' eyes, was the provision in Article I, Section 8, which authorized Congress to raise and support armies. Not content with the power to bleed the states dry financially, the Framers had given the Congress the ultimate means of oppression. A standing army, according to Centinel, is "that grand engine of oppression." And he appeared to have few doubts about the potential willingness of the federal government to use that engine.

The Anti-Federalists viewed both the "general welfare" and the "necessary and proper" clauses of the Constitution with deep suspicion. Centinel asked of the "general welfare" clause, "Now what can be more comprehensive than these words? . . . . The Congress may construe every purpose . . . to be for the general welfare, and thereby seize upon every object of revenue." As for the "necessary and proper" clause, it seemed to be such a sweeping grant of power, the Anti-Federalists could see no logical limits to the powers of the national government. And the arguments of Madison that the federal government was one of enumerated, delegated powers did nothing to reduce their fears on this point.

Their fears were amply confirmed, in their eyes, by the "supremacy clause." Were there any doubts about the end result of ratification of the Constitution in light of this clause? Luther Martin sought to enlighten the voters of Maryland. "[I]f the system is adopted, it will amount to a total and unconditional surrender to that government, by the citizens of this state, of every right and privilege secured to them by our Constitution . . ."

All of these objections reflected the conviction of most Americans in 1787 that men are seldom content to use less power than they are authorized to use. Human beings' lust for power knows no limits. People who are given power will seek to expand and abuse that power. And particularly in the absence of a bill of rights, these provisions of the Constitution seemed especially dangerous.

III. Separation of Powers

An obscure opponent of the Constitution made the following speech at the Virginia Convention:

"That the legislative, executive, and judicial powers should be separate and distinct, is a political fact so well established, that I presume I shall not be thought arrogant when I affirm that no country ever did, or ever can, long remain free, where they are blended. All the states have been in this sentiment when they formed their state constitutions, and therefore have guarded against the danger; and every schoolboy in politics must be convinced of the propriety of the observation; and yet, by the proposed plan, the legislative and executive powers are closely united. . . ."

An opponent in Pennsylvania observed, "This mixture of legislative and executive. . . highly tends to corruption . . . . 'Where the legislative and executive powers (says Montesquieu) are united in the same person, or in the same body of magistrates, there can be no liberty.'"

The Anti-Federalists did not accept Madison's argument that a blending of separated powers was essential if there is to be an effective system of checks and balances. The sharing of power between the president and the Senate in the appointive and treaty-making power simply made the president and Senate "partners in crime." The blending of power meant, for the Anti-Federalists, a breakdown of checks and balances. In Virginia, Patrick Henry, in top form, said, "There will be no checks, no balances in this government. What can avail your specious, imaginary balances, your rope-dancing, chain-rattling, ridiculous ideal checks and contrivances?"

IV. The Congress

The major criticisms of the Congress were the length of terms, re-eligibility for election, and the claim that it would be unrepresentative and aristocratic.

George Clinton of New York wrote, "The most general objections to the first article, [is] that biennial elections for representatives are a departure from the safe democratic principles of annual ones. . ." And the terms of Senators, as well as their mode of selection would lead inevitably to an aristocracy, he added. This view was widely held. The republican principle required, so the Anti-Federalists thought, the representatives of the people to stand for elections every year, or at the very most two years. This was the major means of keeping them responsive to the people.

In addition to frequent elections, rotation in office was important in order to prevent the emergence of a governing class, that is, an aristocracy. By allowing public officials to be re-elected, the Constitution invited corruption in the government. One, or at most, two years was quite enough for any man to be entrusted with power. For once men have tasted power, they develop aristocratic pretensions and become dangerous.

The Constitution provided one representative for every 30,000 inhabitants. The Anti-Federalists believed that it was not possible to represent adequately that many people. And this notion was a result of their view of representative government. The best form of government was one in which men governed themselves, as in a town meeting. This, however, is not practicable, so representative government is necessary. It is a substitute for self-government. It is government by representatives who are authorized to govern on one's behalf. Hence, these representatives should act to the greatest possible degree as the individual citizen would act were he governing himself. This condition was most likely to be realized through frequent elections, ineligibility for re-election, and small electoral districts.

Moreover, a small number of representatives representing large districts, and in the case of senators, entire states, would probably be drawn from the upper classes since only they would have the means and the inclination to run for election. Melancton Smith of New York claimed that few men of the middle class would choose to run for Congress because the office would be "highly elevated and distinguished," the style of living probably "high." Such circumstances would "render the place of a representative not a desirable one to sensible, substantial men, who have been use to walking in the plain and frugal path of life."

This situation described by Smith--the likelihood that the Congress would not be made up of ordinary men--was precisely the opposite of what most Anti-Federalists thought it should be. George Mason said of the representatives that "they ought to mix with the people, think as they think, feel as they feel,--ought to be perfectly amenable to them, and thoroughly acquainted with their interests and conditions." If they were not, there was the danger, according to the Anti-Federalists, of aristocratic domination and the destruction of representative government.

V. The Presidency

Luther Martin warned that a president elected for a four-year term, eligible for re-election, equipped with power to nominate judicial officers, to fill vacancies during the recess of the Senate, to pardon for the offense of treason, and with the armed forces at his disposal would, in fact, be an "elective King." "A King in substance," he would be able, when he chose, to become a "King in name" as well; and if he chose, he could perpetuate the kingship in his family.

George Clinton dwelt with relish on the dissolute ambition, baseness, and perfidy that would characterize the ten square miles of the Federal District. The president would surround himself with "flatterers," "minions and favorites." He would preside over a court that would be an "asylum of the base, idle, avaricious and ambitious." All of this, he concluded, would certainly lead to "a vile and arbitrary aristocracy or monarchy."

The Anti-Federalists, in the lurid pictures they drew of the probable horrors arising from the presiden of
course, reflecting and appealing to the worst fears shared by many Americans as a result of their experie the
British monarchy and the royal governors. While the Federalists were impressed with the need for strong a us
executive leadership, the Anti-Federalists were more impressed with its dangers.

VI. The Judiciary

The Anti-Federalists objected to the absence of a guarantee of trial by jury in civil cases and in crimina at
reach the Supreme Court. They were also convinced that the federal judiciary "would eventually absorb a w
up the state judiciaries. . ." All of this represented a serious threat to the liberties of the people.

Interestingly, not all Anti-Federalists opposed judicial review. Robert Yates of New York preferred the e,
being accountable to the people, to be final governmental interpreter of the Constitution. Patrick Henry b at
the judges in Virginia "opposed the acts of the legislature." He went on, "They had the fortitude to declar y
were the judiciary, and would oppose unconstitutional acts. Are you sure that your federal judiciary will ls
that judiciary as well constructed, and as independent of the other branches, as our state judiciary?" In or
Henry the question was whether the courts as constructed would, not whether they should, exercise the pow i-
cial review.

VII. The Bill of Rights

The issue of the Bill of Rights was the issue on which the Anti-Federalists were victorious. It was as a result
forts that the Bill of Rights was adopted. They were not persuaded by Publius' arguments that a bill of right
necessary to protect the people from a king. Nor did they accept the proposition that the Constitution esta
limited government of enumerated and delegated powers. Many of those delegations of power, they insisted
tremely broad and vague. The "general welfare" and "necessary and proper" clauses as well as the war-makin
were merely a few examples. While it might be true that the Constitution prohibited ex post facto laws,
asked, did it not provide guarantees for other important liberties and rights? These rights are too important
lust for power with which all officeholders are bound to be infected means that the natural rights of the peo
receive specific and extraordinary protection if they are not to be violated.

The fears of the Anti-Federalists and their views of the Constitution adopted in Philadelphia were aptly sum
by Centinel who described that Constitution as the "most daring attempt to establish a despotic aristocrac
freemen, that the world has ever seen."